GOD

didn't

HURT YOU

TIA WILSON

ISBN: 979-8-218-18538-1

TABLE OF CONTENTS

DEDICATION

I dedicate this book to those that have experienced trauma due to a family member, an abuser, an absent parent, a boyfriend, a husband or wife, an imperfect lay member, a prophet, or any leader of a church. If the trauma you experienced has caused you to blame God, this book is for you.

"It hurts trusting God in an area you FEEL He has failed you in… However, the only key to your healing is trusting HIM!!!"

~Tia

INTRODUCTION

You are mad at God and feel hurt by Him because you don't understand why He allowed you to experience heartache and pain; if He's so powerful and knows all things, why didn't He stop it? I understand how you feel. I was mad at God too. If you would, take the time to read about my life and see how God has transformed my pain and suffering into understanding and forgiveness; all so that I may help someone like you. Yes, *you*—the one who purchased this book.

You didn't just pick up this book by mistake. God drew you to this book because He wants to talk to you through my story. He wants to set you free. You may cry, get angry, and/or even laugh while reading my story. You might even be a former abuser, and you keep beating yourself up about what you have done. If so, there is redemption. So, sit down, relax, and get some water, tea, coffee, or a glass of wine. With open ears and hearts, let's see who really hurt you!

Chapter 1

LIFE OF MY YOUTH

Growing up as a little girl in South Central Los Angeles, I remember being one of the worst kids in the neighborhood. I had no respect for adults, and I had no filter. I grew up with my eldest sister and brother. My mother was a workaholic searching for love, which didn't allow her to be home much. But she would make sure I ate before she left home. Man, my mom could cook! She was also a great provider. I don't remember any lights being turned off or ever being hungry.

As a matter of fact, I was one spoiled little girl. I had all the popular kids' clothing brands, the newest toys, and my own furniture. Birthdays and Christmas' were always the best because I knew I was getting everything I asked for.

My big sister was amazing. She would always protect me (when she could) from getting my butt whooped with "Mr. Leather." Yep! That's how my mother referred to the belt she used to whoop me with. She made me get it every time I got in trouble. Even though those whoopings hurt, I was tough and endured them, knowing she would let me go back outside afterward. I know you're probably thinking, "That's a dang shame!" I know, I know, but you know what's funny? I would go right back outside and do whatever I wanted without fear. I may have had an innocent face, but I was as bad as H-E-double-L hockey sticks.

Even though I was a little tomboy who would climb trees and play flag football with the boys, I was very caring. I often got in trouble with my mom because when she bought me new Barbie dolls, I would wrap them up and give them to a friend who couldn't afford any. I always looked out for my friends. I wouldn't let anyone bother them and would even fight boys when needed. I'm telling you, I had no fear. Not even a fear of "Mr. Leather."

One thing I made sure of was no one messed with my friends! I also ensured all my friends knew I was waking them up to walk to mass on Sunday. If they didn't answer their phones, I would go to their houses to ensure they were ready. I would even tell their parents to ensure they woke up, or I would come over and do it myself! It's funny because even though it seemed like I was the worst kid in the neighborhood, I was responsible for ensuring everyone made it to Mass (Catholic Church).

I remember becoming friends with this young lady named Mary, who had just moved to the *Jungles* aka "The J's" (this was the name of our neighborhood), right off Hillcrest and Crenshaw in LA. She was a really bad kid to hang around. I remember she used to have us smoking cigarettes and would allow boys to come to her house when her mother wasn't home.

There is one time in particular that stands out to me. I was at Mary's house doing a craft with scissors when a boy tried to kiss me. When I tried to push him off me, the scissors flew up in the air and landed—edge down—onto my foot. To this day, I still have a scar to prove it. He had me *twisted*! I wasn't playing about him kissing me. Plus, I was interested in someone else and *not him*!

After that drama, Mary and I fell out over time because she was a little older than me. Mary was a bully. One day, I remember we were at the open lot off of Santo Tomas in the Jungles. As a young girl, I had long pigtails that hung all the way to my butt. On this particular day, I had my hair in two pigtails. Mary and I were hanging out playing in the open field (now called the Baldwin Hills Park). Out of nowhere, Mary grabbed one of my ponytails and swung me around one good time. That *hurt*! Then, she had the nerve to throw my shoe into this big nasty trash can! With tears in my eyes, I told her I was going to tell. After that, I ran home to tell my mama. When I entered the house, my mama asked me, "What's wrong with you?" I told her how Mary swung me around by my ponytail and threw my shoe in the trash. Then my mama said, "Do you know where she lives?" I said, "Yes," and took her to Mary's house.

When my mom and I walked up the hill to Mary's house, we knocked on her door. Mary's mother answered, and my mother told her that Mary better not put her hands on me again! My mama didn't play when it came to me, and she was far from being scared of anyone. Mary's mom was livid, and she apologized for Mary's actions. As we were walking back to our house, we overheard yelling. When we turned around, we saw Mary's mother beating her with a mop. I told my mom, "That's what she gets for being a bully." Then my mom looked at me and said, "Don't say that," as we walked back to the apartment. It was at that moment I decided I would never be bullied again.

To protect myself from being bullied, I started watching boxing on Select TV to learn how to fight. I would watch very intensely, then ask my guy friends to play fight because I wanted to practice what I saw. I loved watching Sugar Ray Lennard. He was one of my favorite boxers. Eventually, I became really good at boxing. That confidence added to my not fearing anyone. And I mean, *no one.*

At this time, I still didn't have a filter and no respect for adults. I would cuss ya mama, sista, daddy, brother, whomever out, and go back home and tell my mama I did it. I never lied about anything I did. I have to admit that I was quite a handful. On the one hand, I was very smart in school. But on the other hand, I got in trouble *a lot*—especially when I attended St. Bernadette. If someone mistreated me, or if one of the nuns tried to hit me with that wooden board with holes, I would look at them and say, "If you hit me, I'm hitting you back!" If I deserved to be spanked, I would take the beating without complaints. But if, for one minute, a nun—shoot anyone—

thought they would whoop me for something I didn't do, I would fight back.

That was my mindset: if they hit me, I would hit them back. This mindset didn't just apply to school; I acted the same way at home. For example, I recall when my sister threatened to whoop me with a belt in her hand. I told her, "If you do, I'mma go get a belt and hit you back!" She looked at me with this serious look, but I looked back at her just as seriously. Then, she shook her head at me and walked away. Soon after that, she started calling me "the bad seed."

My tantrums with my sister didn't stop there. I would spit, kick, and attempt to swing on her friends if I didn't like them. They would hold my head at arms-length and laugh, asking my sister, "What's wrong with your little sister?" Her reply would be, "Bad as hell." She hated taking me anywhere with her, but she had to because my mother was usually at work or on her love journey. So, my sister had to watch me. I remember begging my sister to take me with her, promising I wouldn't tell mama her business. She would take me, and sure enough, when mama came home, I would tell all her business! Man, I was a trip LOL!

Despite how I misbehaved at times, I loved my big sister. She was like my mother, and my brother was like my father. See, my mom and dad were together just long enough to have me, and then they divorced. My siblings' father wasn't my dad. My father was a great dad when he was sober. He became an alcoholic when I was just a young girl. He came from a perfect, loving mother and father (who, by the way, was Bishop Emmanuel Wilson Sr. of the Church of God and Christ). My father had a healthy upbringing. He had no reason to abuse substances. However, it all started when he started hanging out with some friends that smoked weed. One day, they decided to lace their weed with cocaine. This is how my father was introduced to cocaine and became addicted.

My mom only allowed me to see my dad when I got older. I remember my dad driving to my school and waiting for me to start walking home so he could see me. He did this quite often. I never got in the car with him, but he would talk to me while I was walking home. I don't remember when, but shortly after, I was able to spend time with my dad and visit my grandmother on 57th Street (east side of Los Angeles). I met some new friends there and my other two brothers (my dad's sons from his first marriage).

I got along with both of my brothers and loved them dearly, but the youngest and I used to get into it occasionally. As much as we had our loving moments, he used to provoke me and therefore got me in trouble. For example, I remember he kept annoying me by getting in my face. I would ask him to move and he wouldn't. I got fed up with him antagonizing me and took matters into my own hands.

One day, as he was provoking me as usual, I looked down and guess what I saw on the floor? A thick rubber band. I told him if he didn't get out of my face, I would pop the rubber band in his eye. Well, you know what? He didn't believe me. So...

POP! I did it, and it went straight into his eye. He went off crying and hollering to my dad, saying, "She popped me in the eye with a rubber band!" I told my dad, "Well, he kept provoking me. I told him if he didn't stop, I was going to hit him in the eye with the rubber band but he didn't listen. So, I did it!"

Man, my dad gave me a serious butt-whooping. It was much more painful than the spanking I was used to from him. See, my dad had two boys. I was, and still am, dad's little girl. So, the beating didn't just hurt my butt—it also hurt my feelings. I was so mad at my brother for getting me in trouble. However, despite our challenges, he really meant a lot to me, even today.

Hanging out at my dad's house was fun for the most part. My brothers lived with their mom, but they often visited our dad. At this time, my dad didn't disappear. Instead, he just smoked a lot of weed. Well, maybe he was gone, but I didn't notice because I was at the neighbor's house, on the other side of my brother's grandmother's house. This is also where my brother's girlfriend, Alice, lived. Alice became like family to our neighbors who lived across the street from my dad and me. Alice's grandmother lived down the street from my grandmother on 67th street off Broadway.

My dad and I often ate breakfast at my grandmother's house. I even hung out with her sometimes. While there, I learned etiquette and how to set the table. My grandmother didn't want anyone in her refrigerator unless you asked, and she made that clear. There were a lot of rules at grandma's house. You couldn't play cards because she thought it was gambling. You couldn't use her phone and had to go to bed when she did. Man, I was like, "Can I be a kid here?" LOL. The only thing I enjoyed about being there was that Grandma Wilson cooked her butt off! She made the best homemade tea. She would put tea bags in a water pitcher, add fresh lemons from her tree in the backyard, and then place them in the sun. Man, that was the best sun tea I've ever tasted. It was sooo good. And don't get me started on the *bomb* peach cobbler she used to prepare. She always made the dough with love and flavored those peaches just right. Grandma could darn right cook. *Period*! Best cook, hands down.

I don't ever remember eating at my dad's house. We always had breakfast and dinner at Grandma Wilson's house. However, my dad often took me to this small bar right off Crenshaw. I was the only child ever present there. I used to think it was cool because I got all the attention and free *7UP*. Though we were in a bar, I never recall my dad being drunk. He may have had a few drinks and played pool, but I never saw him exceed his limit. Although, when it came to weed, my dad would often chop it up, and get his little white paper ready to roll up a joint. He would keep his weed in a cigar box, and even though he never smoked in front of me, he had no issue rolling one up.

I remember his girlfriend would come by the house with a much older son than me. When she and my dad went out, my dad would leave me home with her son, not knowing any better. I hated staying at the house with him because he wouldn't let me go outside to play with my friends. Instead, he would make me look at Playboy (porn) and force me to do what he saw in the magazines...

Eventually, my dad stopped seeing that woman. I could not have been happier because that meant I would no longer have to dread them going out and me having to stay at home with her son. That was the only time—outside of when my dad would have disappearing acts—that I hated being at my dad's house. Once, he disappeared for days, and I had to eat across the street and get my next-door neighbor to do my hair. Outside of my dad's addiction, I really enjoyed spending time with him. My dad was cool, funny, and fun, yet also a disciplinarian. If I came to his house with makeup, he would make me take it off. He told me I was too young to wear makeup (and he was right).

I was in the 5th grade then, and would play with my mom's makeup while she was at work. See, my dad would get me when my mom was gone. And in most cases, my brother and sister were gone too. I would sneak into my mother's room, try on her makeup, and put on her heels. My mom had the cutest shoes with her little feet. I would have so much fun wearing them around the house— until I thought she was on her way home, LOL!

There's such a big age gap between my siblings and me. My brother is nine years older than me, and my sister is eleven years older. I had so much fun with them, except when my brother decided to practice karate with me and tore Henry's arm. Henry was my Snoopy-looking bear. I always carried him and a blanket while sucking my thumb; that was how I got the nickname "Linus" from the cartoon Snoopy. I was so attached to that blanket that my sister had to ask me to let her wash it. When I finally said yes, I never saw that blanket again. That was just *wrong*. Hahaha! After that, I stopped sucking my thumb.

Since I was the baby of the family and my mom was a workaholic, I often stayed with my sister. My brother left to live with his dad while I was just a young girl living in the Jungle of Los Angeles, Ca. Sometimes my brother would come and get me, spend time with me, and spoil me. I used to love hanging out with my brother. He was so fun to be around. We laughed a lot, and he showered me with love. He had wealthy friends that loved his lil' sister too. So much so they would come to pick me up from school in either a Porsche, Mercedes, or Rolls-Royce. His friends had adopted me as their little sister as well.

I had so much fun with my brother; I looked up to him. He always had nice things. He was funny and caring and gave me anything I wanted. See, my desire to get more out of life came from my brother. Now don't get me wrong. My mother bought me name-brand clothes, toys, and eel-skin shoes—she was very good at that. However, my brother introduced me to golf and the finer things of life. He would always take me to my favorite Cuban restaurant on Venice Blvd, in LA—especially on my birthday. It was *our thing*. My sister, brother, and I did that every year until my sister left for the Airforce and my brother got busy with work and life. This was when life started getting really rough for me. I was a popular girl with many friends, but my home life was becoming more challenging. It all started when we moved from Santo Tomas to Oceanside due to my mother's job. I had been going to St. Bernadette since kindergarten, and now I was in the fourth grade moving to another city.

Right before moving, I had a really good friend that lived down the street. His name was Hasanni, and he was Iranian and Indian. He became my male best friend. We would hang tight with each other. For example, I was the only one who could wake him up for school in the morning. He wasn't scared of anything or anybody—not even the police. Before moving to Oceanside, Hasanni went to see his dad in Iran. When he came back, he convinced his mom to ask my mom if he could take me out on a chaperoned date. She said yes!

I remember getting ready that night and waiting for him to pick me up. It didn't take him long because he lived only two minutes from me. I was so nervous and excited all at the same time. While waiting intensely, I looked out the window and saw a limo pulling up to our apartment. I was in such awe like; this is *for me*? I had such a huge smile on my face.

The driver opened the door, and my Hassani and his mother came out of the limo. As they walked towards my door, I just stood there in awe. Hasanni was such a gentleman. But wait, that wasn't all! We drove to the restaurant, and I remember going inside. There was an area blocked off just for us to have a candlelight dinner. After we ate, Hasanni surprised me with a gift from Iran. Inside was a nice necklace. I was so excited about it and so thankful.

Overall, that night was memorable. Hasanni's mom really outdid herself. She was very loving and treated me like part of her family. Occasionally, she would take me with them on family outings. She even would take me on base with her. Yeah, Hassani's mom was in the military. I believe this is how she met his father.

I also really loved Hassani's grandmother. She was sooo funny and would *tell it like it is.* She was a very, very caring and a loving woman as well. Hassani's family was so good to me. After moving, I lost touch with Hasanni for a short time but eventually reconnected. Present day, he is doing well and married with two children. We still check on each other from time to time.

My relationship with my mother suffered when we moved from the Jungles to Oceanside. I started resenting her. It was like when my brother and sister moved away from home. At that point, my life started becoming more challenging. My mother and I didn't get along. I'll never forget when she told me she was tired of taking care of me. She said it was time to live her life; it was my father's turn to look after me. I was in the sixth grade at the time.

Can you imagine that? My dad, an alcoholic and an addict, was about to start taking care of me. How was that going to work? It wasn't like my mama didn't know that my dad was an addict. This was not a secret. I must admit that my dad really tried to be there for me. I remember he enrolled me in 61st Street School on the Eastside of LA. I wasn't sure about meeting new friends, but I did. I made a friend (my twin), whom everyone thought was related to me because we looked so much alike. Then I gained another friend named Shawna.

Shawna and I became best friends, although we bumped heads at first. She was the drill team captain, and I was also determined to become one—to the extent that I practiced all the time until I perfected the routines. Eventually, I auditioned to be the second captain and got the position. That was a proud moment for me. After that day, Shawna and I gradually became the best of friends. She was like a sister to me. Her mom was the best, and her Aunty Cookie...man, I loved her Auntie. She used to take us to the horse track so she could bet on her horses, she was so much fun. I miss Shawna, she was my ride-or-die.

Though I liked being with my dad, I didn't have a lot of friends. There weren't a lot of kids my age near my daddy's house on 57th Street. All my friends lived in the J's, and I missed hanging out with them. We would play double-dutch there quite a bit. My sister (well, we called each other sisters), Donna, had a drill team squad she used to lead, and I would help her with the routines. This kept us involved in our community in a positive way. Well, let me speak for myself because Donna was a Blood (gang member). However, she had a mothering spirit and was well known in the J's.

It was only a short time before I got acclimated to my new elementary school. My dad didn't play when it came to my education. Shoot, I remember when he yelled at me for folding my school paper. He told me that folded papers would not be accepted when I went to college. I looked at him like, "Daddy, I'm only in the sixth grade!" Nonetheless, he made me write that paper all over again. I will never forget that moment.

I had been living with my dad for some time as I was promoted to drill team captain alongside Shawna. I remember being so excited about my school's drill team being in the parade. I used to always be in parades with my dad High (my brother and sister's father), but just sitting in a car, waving my hand, and being cute, LOL. However, our drill team had uniforms, and I could show out instead of sitting pretty in a car. We wore cold-white outfits with tap-white boots with shingles on them. You couldn't tell us *nathing*!!!

Shawna and I had *the big head*. Let me tell you, we worked that street like we owned it. We had some *bad* drummers and a *bomb* beat. Our drill team was *cold*. That year, we won first place, and I won a medal as captain, working my *stuff*. As I said, you couldn't tell me *nathing*! The only thing was that neither of my parents were present to see how happy I was. Their absences were always disappointing.

By the time I turned thirteen, it seemed like all hell had broken loose in my life. Even though I was having fun being with my friends and enjoying school, I was silently experiencing tremendous trauma and the loss of my best friend. You see, one Friday night, Shawna and her mother were on their way to get me so we could go skating at *World on Wheels*. We did this every Friday. However, one night, they took longer than usual. I started getting concerned and said to my mom. "I hope everything is okay…" My mom tried to stay as positive as she could.

The night started getting later and later, and I hadn't heard anything from Shawna or her mother. *Nothing.* We didn't have cell phones back then, so I couldn't call. She never called that night to let me know she couldn't pick me up. I felt very numb and didn't know why. The next day, I remembered having Shawna's Aunty Cookie's number written down. I decided to give her a call. The phone rang, and when she answered, I said, "Hello, Aunty Cookie? She said, "Hello? Who is this?" I said, "Danyle. She said, "Shawna's bestfriend Danyle?" I said, "Yes." There was a small silence, and I felt my heart drop.

Finally, I said, "What happened?" She asked if anyone had called me, and I replied, "No." That was when Aunt Cookie said, "Baby, I am so sorry, but they were hit by a drunk driver last night. Shawna didn't have her seatbelt on. She flew out of the window and died instantly. Her mom is in ICU due to her busting her head on the window." I was devastated by the news! I blamed myself for this happening to her. All of this had happened because they were on the way to pick me up…that hurt my heart so bad.

Not only did I lose my best friend, but I was also molested by those closest to me. Once by a family member's girlfriend's sister. And finally, by two other family members when I was thirteen. The latter was one of my most traumatizing experiences. During this time, my two family members got me drunk and high. They made me get on my knees and socked me in my head several times. From there, they made me give them blow jobs. Later that night, the older one waited until I was asleep and snuck into my bedroom. I was still drunk when he started touching my vagina, telling me to be quiet. I was terrified.

When I told my other family members what had happened, they said I was lying and making a mockery. I was embarrassed and humiliated. Later on, my father went on a binge and left me home for three days. Once again, I had to eat across the street and get my hair combed by my brother's girlfriend, who was my dad's neighbor. When my dad finally returned home, he kept apologizing for leaving me alone. He cried and apologized for leaving me home like that.

Not too long after my dad came home, I saw my brother, T, pulling up in front of my dad's house. I ran outside to greet him. He walked up to the porch and told me to get my things because he was taking me back to mom's house. I went to grab my things, kissed my dad goodbye, and hopped in my brother T's car. He drove me to mom's house and dropped me off.

I didn't want to go back to mom's house. I ran away a few times due to not feeling loved by my mom. This void caused me to adapt to street life (survival), and my friends became my family. I was free in the streets. I was a teenager that participated in many community drill teams, went hiking with friends, and went to the movies often—as long as I was in before the streetlights came on.

When it came to school, my mother took me to a school out of town because she thought it would keep me off the streets. Our relationship wasn't great. For example, when I turned thirteen, my mother refused to take me to my graduation or buy my outfit. I couldn't believe she was doing this to me, especially since I had worked so hard to graduate with extra credit.

Back then, I promised my mom I wouldn't get into fights at school. However, the one fight I did get into, wasn't at school. I took it to the park…LOL. I told my mom about this fight in advance because I was being picked on at school. Apparently, this girl didn't like me but wanted to fight because she feared me. Her name was Shell. Shell had lied and told another girl (that everyone was scared of because she was from a set (gang)) that I was talking about her mother. Yet, *she* was the one actually doing that. Shell had Alla and the rest of their little click fooled. She often had the girls throw salad and cans at me while I walked through the hallway. This was all in an attempt to provoke me. She was just being messy. I would tell them not to let me catch them by themselves away from school one by one.

Finally, I got tired of this and called ole girl Alla and said, "Look if you want to fight me, meet me at the park. I'm not going to let you stop me from graduating." She then replied, "I was told *you* wanted to fight *me*." I said, "Who told you that?"

Anyone who knows me knows I don't have a problem telling someone if I have an issue with them. It would never come through a third party; it would come straight from my mouth. I told Alla that Shell was the one talking about her mother. So, we set Shell up at the park. We made Shell think Alla was meeting me at the park to fight me. However, both Alla and I pretended like we were going to fight. While Shell was right in the middle of us in staging the fight...bam! There it went, my fist to Shell's face. I started confronting her about her lie, and we took turns whooping her butt. It was so bad her mom called the police and pressed charges against me.

Another young lady that was a part of Alla's squad had a problem with me. She told me her homegirl was going to the school to kill me. Unfortunately, she died in a car wreck on her way to my school. Now mind you, we were only eighth graders. All this was done to me because I was pretty, not a liar, and I wasn't scared of anyone. *If you don't want the truth, don't ask me.* Everyone knew not to gossip around me because I learned really early that is how you get your name in the middle of stuff. I hated when people would say something I didn't say. I started telling the gossipers that if they didn't want me to go back and tell so-n-so what they said, don't come to me with it. And, if I had to, I would go grab the person they were talking about and tell them to say it to their face because I wasn't going to get caught in their mess.

To this day, I never understood why my mother wasn't excited about my accomplishment or why it didn't matter to her how old the guys I dated were. I was dating Rick, a 19-year-old guy, whom I met while hanging out at my best friend Dee's house. I started dating him before he had any money. He was a pretty cool guy and fun. During our dating period, Rich inherited some money and spoiled a sista. Here I am, an eighth grader pulling up in a red Benz, hair done, nails done, and dressing *fly*. We hung out for quite some time until he started becoming really jealous and fighting me occasionally.

One night, off of the Crenshaw/Florence area, I had walked down a block from my apartment to see Rich and my homegirls. They were at my best friend Dee's aunty's house. I had decided to break up with Rich that night. I wasn't tolerating Rich hitting on me anymore. Little did I know we would argue over a lie my best friend's sister Minny had told him. She and I were cool but not *that* cool. We both had an eye for Rich, and we both knew it. Some time before, I approached her and said, "Let us both pursue him and let him choose who he wants to be with. Once Rich makes his choice, the other one has to back off. Deal?" Minny said, "Deal."

See, Minny had the body, and I had the long hair with a body of a pencil and a little junk in the trunk. Go ahead and laugh at me...I was still cute! Minny never let that go. She would laugh when he and I fought and she talked about me. The fights were always at my best friend Dee's house since this is where everyone hung out, and it was my second home. However, she saw an opportunity to find a way for us to break up by giving Rich some false information about me hooking up with some boy at my school. He and I were clowning to make his girl jealous. I didn't date my home boys as that was a violation. Minny started a mess over nothing.

I almost lost my life behind a lie. Rich and I started arguing, and I wasn't backing down from him. Eventually, I got tired of arguing and yelled, "I don't want to be with you anymore." He gave me this death look and said, "What did you say?" With a strong attitude and twisted face, I repeated, "I DON'T WANT TO BE WITH YOU anymore!!!" He grabbed me by my throat and choked me until I passed out. When he finally let me go, I fell straight back from the top of the curb, hit the ground, and busted my head open on the street. I blacked out for a minute or two before I came to myself. Once I opened my eyes, all I could feel was him kicking me and yelling; he was telling me to get up. I eased up slowly from off the ground, not knowing the condition of my head. No one watching called for help while this was happening. I touched the back of my head, and all I could feel was blood. Blood was running down my back. I looked at him and said I need help. I had blood running down my head. He gave me a long stare and let me go.

It was at that point that I ran to get help. I went back to my house, told my mother what had happened, and begged her not to call my brother T because I didn't want him to go to jail for murder. My brother would have killed him. She promised not to tell my brother T and gave me a towel to hold my head while driving me to the emergency room. It wasn't bad enough for me to get stitches. Thank God! However, they cut my hair to treat the wound and bandaged me. I had to walk around with gauze wrapped around my head for a while. All this was because I didn't want to be with Rich anymore.

Y'all ready for this? Do you know Rich still wasn't done with me? You would have thought he had done enough damage already. A few days after the incident, I visited my best friend, Dee. While there, Rich pulled up to the house. No one was at the house except Dee and myself. Dee looked at me and said, "You want me to let him in?" I said, "That's fine, maybe he wants to apologize." Dee let Rich in the house. As she walked back to sit on the couch, Rich looked at me, pulled out a 22-millimeter gun, sat down, then took out all the bullets and kept one inside. He spun the barrel, got up, and pointed the gun at me. I started running around the house as he was pulling the trigger but no bullet. I finally stopped running, turned around, and told him, "If you're going to shoot me, just shoot me because I'm not running away from you anymore!" By this time, we were back in the front, where Dee could see us while sitting on the couch in the living room.

He looked at my best friend Dee and asked her if she would tell if he shot me. She paused for a moment looking at him like, *are you serious!?* Then she looked at my face and loudly replied, "Hell yeah, I'll tell on you if you shoot her!" Realizing Dee was serious, he put the gun down. Then he said, "You're lucky she said 'Yea.'" Shortly after that incident, he went to jail for robbing a pizza place.

Chapter 2

LIFE TURNED UPSIDE DOWN

I met a guy at the Dorsey pool during my ninth-grade summer. He was a fine lifeguard, and he thought I was fine too. He hollered at a sista, and we exchanged numbers. Little did he know I wasn't an easy catch. I actually threw away his number right after we met. Guys would always try to talk to me because I was a pretty girl with long hair. I dressed well and took very good care of myself. So, meeting a fine man was nothing out of the ordinary to me. However, Mr. Lifeguard was older and very charming.

Not long after meeting this amazing Mr. Lifeguard, my mom took me and Dee (my best friend) to Las Vegas for *Circus Circus*. While there, we met these guys that spoiled us like crazy. We came home with their numbers, the stuffed animals they had given us, and some money in our pockets. At that point, I wasn't thinking anything about Mr. Lifeguard.

Sometime after we returned from Vegas, I ran into him again. I was sitting at the bus stop waiting to catch my bus when he pulled up in his white low-rider truck (spray painted on the side with a nice design). He asked if he could take me home, and I answered, "No. I can catch the bus (with my smart mouth)." He replied, "Come on, why don't you let me take you home?" I said, "Because I can catch the bus. I'm good." After sitting there for about ten minutes with him not giving up, I finally agreed to let him take me home. This experience was the beginning of my first lesson in real love.

Mr. Lifeguard took me on a few dates. He wined and dined me very well—he was a complete gentleman. After dating for a few months, I started to really like Mr. Lifeguard. He was about three years older than me and had a great head on his shoulders. He was fine, athletic, goal-oriented, and had a good job. Even though I had a lot of guy friends that used to gang bang and slang (sell drugs), I wouldn't talk to them. I didn't date those who banged, and if you slang dope, you had to have a plan on when you would stop. Plus, I didn't date any of my home boys.

Mr. Lifeguard was fine, smart, and had a lil roughneck in him. He had also had his share of women. I didn't care about that because I wasn't trying to be with him like that. In fact, I was getting to know a couple of guys myself, LOL. I remember Mr. Lifeguard was smooth and could kiss really well. Ummm hmmm, I loved Mr. Lifeguard's kisses. So much so that it almost got me into bed with him, but I would never give in. See, Mr. Lifeguard thought I was going to be easy breezy. He felt if he wined and dined me, I would give him some *nookie!* Hahahahaha…well, little did he know, I wasn't easy.

Once he learned this, I then became a challenge for him. Mr. Lifeguard started really liking me. He had no idea he would fall in love—with a bet. Oooh, yeah! I later learned that Mr. Lifeguard had bet his friends that he would get some of my nookie very quickly. And how did I find this out? Well, Mr. Lifeguard told me the truth one Friday at my house. He came by my place off Crenshaw and Florence bearing gifts. While there, he sneaked a pager into my bag and called it. I remember thinking, what's that noise? I looked for it, and sure enough, he had bought me a pager, some bamboo earrings I wanted, and let me wear his fat link chain (that he knew I loved). I was like, 'This is sweet of him!' This was his way of asking me to be his girl.

Being official with Mr. Lifeguard meant I would have to let my lil "friends"—the side pieces I had been talking to all along—go. I wasn't ready to do that yet, so I told him I couldn't be his girl. I didn't feel bad about denying his request either. See, I knew that Mr. Lifeguard was a player, and I refused to date a player. I was territorial, hot-headed, and wasn't sharing my man with anyone.

Mr. Lifeguard was spoiled by his mom, yet he was also very hard-working. When I met him, he stayed with his mom; they were tight. His mom was extremely supportive. She allowed him to stay with her until he saved up enough money for a down payment on a house (which was rare for an African American mother to do back in the day). I really admired that about her. She and Mr. Lifeguard truly had a great relationship.

However, she did not like me, his ex, or any of his other female or guy friends. She told me to my face that she thought I was too young for her son.

The day after I declined to be Mr. Lifeguard's girl, I got really sick. I was throwing up and just not feeling well. I felt it was because I had turned down his offer, so I called him. When he answered the phone, I told him I would be his girlfriend under one condition: he would have to let all those other women go and stop wearing khakis. He agreed, and this was where our journey of love began.

I must say, Mr. Lifeguard was my *everything*. He was my best friend. We did everything together, from lifting weights to playing on a co-ed softball team. Softball is one sport I love playing. First base, shortstop, and third base were my positions. Being with him always felt natural. Whether or not I wanted his opinion, he was very honest with me. I loved many things about him, but most importantly, I valued his belief in me.

At this time, I remember my mom stopped giving me lunch money and buying my school clothes. I had guy friends that would provide me with money or anything I needed. *No strings.* These were the same guys I had play-fought with back in the day, so they respected me because I fought and was as brave as one of the homies. I was off limits.

Dating guys that took care of me and spoiled me was my norm. However, Mr. Lifeguard and I had a bumpy start. His ex was upset because he didn't choose to settle down with her. His mother didn't approve of me because I was so young. He was getting called all kinds of names. Females would leave messages on his voicemail saying I was jailbait and he ought to be ashamed of himself for dating me. On top of all of that, his mother wasn't welcoming when I came over.

Then I had dudes mad lying about me to Mr. Lifeguard because I didn't want to be with them. I remember calling this dude on the three-way and telling him to meet me at the corner and say what he said to my face. As I stated in the other chapter, I could not stand for someone to say I did or said something I didn't. That was and still is one of my biggest pet peeves. One thing I wasn't was a liar!

Mr. Lifeguard didn't know what to believe, so we took a short time-out, and that is when I realized how much I cared about him. He gave me everything I wanted but not when I asked for it—I loved this about him. We always blessed each other on birthdays, Valentine's Day, and Christmas. He encouraged me to get a job. He started talking to me about college. God had given me what I needed and yearned for.

We had some rocky roads. One of my roughest times was when I caught him cheating on me. I remember I was partying at UCLA with my girls when I felt something in my gut. I told them, "Hey, we need to go. Mr. Lifeguard is doing something he doesn't have any business doing." My girls knew how I rolled and asked if they needed to roll with me. I told them, "Naw, I got it." We got in the car, and I took them home. Then, I headed over to Mr. Lifeguard's house.

I pulled up, and what do you know? An unrecognized car was sitting in front of his house. We had been dating for about two years at that point. We were like Bonnie and Clyde. Everywhere you saw him, you saw me. We had some time apart with our friends too. We had broken up, but y'all know that back in the day, you can say you broke up, but you're still together, and you better not see them with anyone??? LMBO… don't leave me hanging out here by myself. Hahahaha! But anyway, it was like 12:30 am when I pulled up to his house. I walked to his window, and heard my tape (that I gave him) playing, with music we used to listen to while making love.

At this point, I was hurt, but really, really calm. He turned on the light, and what do I see with my own eyes?! A head bobbing up and down. I knocked on his door, and he answered. He hurried up and came to the door. I ask him to let me in, and he goes, "Why? To beat her up?" I said no. I told Mr. Lifeguard to tell her to get up, put her clothes on, and go home NOW!!

In the meantime, Mr. Lifeguard asked me to go home. I said okay. You think I went home? No!!! I got into my step dad's car and made the block. I threw a flashlight at her window shield when I made a block. Thank God it didn't break her window. She walked outside and started talking noise. I told him to tell her to shut up, get into her car, and go home. I wasn't talking to her, yet she kept on.

Mind you, my car was still running during this time, but it was a stick shift. So, he walked up to me because she kept talking crazy, and he saw me about to run up on her. She kept talking, so I ran back to jump into my car and run her over. Mr. Lifeguard grabbed me and had to drop kick me on the grass (because I was too strong), to keep me from doing anything crazy to her. Luckily she got in her car and left. He kept saying, "Before you leave me," and I would say, "I'm not going to leave you, but why would you do this to me," with tears running down my face. He started apologizing to me, and we went into the house and made some good love. I guess it was that good makeup lovin' that got me pregnant that night…

Back then, I was only sixteen-years-old. I had no clue I was pregnant. One day, while we were sitting on her bed eating a big mixing bowl of cereal like two possibly pregnant women, my best friend stated that she didn't have her cycle, and our cycle came at the same time. She and I both took a home pregnancy test, and PREGNANT we were. I was so afraid I didn't know what to do. I told Mr. Lifeguard, and he told his mother. That was the end of *that*. She already didn't like me; now I was pregnant. She wasn't having that.

My mother had no clue I was pregnant. I remember it was a Friday morning. Lifeguard's mom made an appointment for me to have an abortion without discussing it with my mother. That was so hard to do. I remember being so afraid. I didn't want to go through with the abortion, but I felt I had no choice. That's one mistake I wish I had never made. Going into that dark room and seeing a trash can underneath me for them to throw the fetus away in traumatized me. I will never forget it.

Just the thought of what happened that day still brings tears to my eyes.

After the procedure, Mr. Lifeguard's mom took me back to the house with her. I called my mother and told her I was staying at Mr. Lifeguard's house for the weekend, and she said ok. I was in excruciating pain. I remember Mr. Lifeguard said he would never take anyone else through that heartache. I couldn't sleep at night because I was in so much pain and sorrow—a choice had been made for me. I didn't know any better. However, I'm glad that Mr. Lifeguard loved me through it.

After that weekend, Mr. Lifeguard apologized for making me go through that. I really felt that moment brought us closer as a couple and as friends. That was one thing about Mr. Lifeguard and me: we could talk to each other about anything. We were very open with each other. We went through some ups and downs, but our love and friendship got us through.

Mr. Lifeguard really believed in me. He knew how much I wanted to be a model. He visited me one day and asked if he approached my mother and asked her to go half with him to pay for a photo shoot, would she do it? I said, "I don't know. Ask her." Mr. Lifeguard asked my mother, and she agreed to go half on my photos. I was so excited and started pursuing my dream of becoming a famous model.

Mr. Lifeguard took me to Top Model agency in downtown LA where they scheduled a photographer for me to shoot with. While I was out doing my photoshoot, a lady from Seventeen

Magazine saw me and gave me her number. She told me to come see her when my photos came back. I looked at Mr. Lifeguard, smiling from ear to ear with excitement! OMG, I was so excited; I was crazy, happy, and excited. A few weeks later, Top Model told me my negatives were ready to pick up. Mr. Lifeguard took me to look at my photos when they came in, and we called the lady from Seventeen Magazine to let her know my negatives had arrived.

I set an appointment to see her, and Mr. Lifeguard took me there, knowing she was also a scout for Jet Magazine and Ebony Fashion fair. Man, the dreams of my life were about to happen. At least, I thought. I was an underage minor, and Mr. Lifeguard wasn't a legal guardian, so he couldn't sign for me, which really sucked. My mother worked, and couldn't take me downtown to sign a contract with Seventeen Magazine. She just didn't have the time.

Come to find out that she and my step dad had decided to move to Oklahoma at the end of my junior year of High School at Dorsey high, where all my friends attended school. I thought to myself, "Are you kidding me right now? I'm right at the break of my modeling career! My dream is being fulfilled!" These are the thoughts that crossed my mind. I just needed my mom to drive downtown to the modeling agency. Unbelievable…

This is where devastation after devastation happened. My mother never signed the contract. She made me sell my Plush Bug (Volkswagen) I had purchased for myself with the money I had received from a car wreck I was in. My mom promised to buy me another car when we moved to Oklahoma. So, I sold it in the hopes of getting a new one. I just didn't want to leave. I was thinking of ways I could stay in LA. I didn't want to leave Mr. Lifeguard, all my friends, and my career. This was all too hurtful.

One day, my sister informed me that she would take over mom's apartment that we lived in. Really?? Great to know! I convinced my sister to let me stay with her and let mom go to Oklahoma. My big sister came back to LA after serving her time in the Air Force. She wanted to move into the area my mom, and I lived in. You would think I would be excited about staying with my sister. However, I was bitter about not being able to sign up with Seventeen Magazine. I was angry because my mom didn't sign my modeling contract before she left. I was already a hothead, but not being able to fulfill my dream made me worse.

I was just a little too feisty and spoiled. For example, I skunk off one day from my sister to get a tattoo. Mr. Lifeguard and I were getting into it often. I remember being so mad at him that I attempted to walk to his house from Manchester in Hillcrest to Gardena at midnight without a fear in my bones. I was so mad. I remember walking to 108th and Crenshaw and saw a couple of police officers at the donut shop (of course) getting donuts and coffee. I approached the officers and asked if they could give me a ride home. I told them my friends got mad because I wouldn't drink or smoke with them and dropped me off at the corner to walk home. Just lying! Oh, they believed me. I had them drop me off at Mr. Lifeguards' house. Yep right in his driveway. I thanked the officers, walked to Mr. Lifeguard's door, and knocked on it. He opened the door and said, "Go back home." I said I couldn't. Mr. Lifeguard said, "Why not?" I responded, "Because I walked to 108th, saw the police at the donut shop, told them a lie, and asked them to drop me off at home." He looked out the door, saw the police in the driveway, and let me in.

Mr. Lifeguard said, "You walked here?" With this little snicker he used to do and a laugh. I said yes. Then I told him how I got the police to do it. This is the night Mr. Lifeguard realized how much I loved him. I also discovered I loved him and didn't want to lose or be without him. After this had happened, we had a really good heart-to-heart about this move to Oklahoma. Mr. Lifeguard wasn't ready to move out of his mother's house and be responsible for me. He hadn't saved up enough to buy a house and he had refused to rent an apartment.

Mr. Lifeguard suggested I go to Oklahoma, finish school, and go to college while he saved up for us to have a home. To show me he meant what he said, he took me to the jewelry store and bought me a promise ring as a reminder that we were going to get married. He just wanted me to finish high school and college so we could both have our careers and be successful. Mr. Lifeguard was far from average and only moved above the average with no fear. However, the only thing he feared was airplanes yet he also promised to get on one to come and see me. This is how I knew he really loved me.

He went as far as telling my mom when she came back to get the rest of our things that he would help her drive to Oklahoma and fly back home. I looked at him and said, "For real?? Are you serious? Just for me? He sure did. When my mom returned to LA to get the rest of our things and me, (I was too much for my sister to handle), Mr. Lifeguard packed a bag, and we hit the highway. He drove my mother and me to Oklahoma. Now, he almost killed us by falling asleep behind the wheel. However, we made it to Oklahoma safe and sound. Then, Mr. Lifeguard flew back to Los Angeles.

Chapter 3:

THE START OF OKLAHOMA

Mr. Lifeguard went back home and left me in the straight country. Talk about being traumatized... OMG! I felt like I had just walked into *a nightmare on no street.* Morris, Oklahoma had no street lights, sidewalks, gas stations, corner stores, or *nathan*!!! You hear me?! It was dark outside due to the lack of street lights. You couldn't even see your hands. Well, I may be exaggerating a little, but man, it was pitch to the black dark. We had a shotgun in the house because you could never see who was approaching your front door at night. Then to top it off, we lived around a bunch of INSECTS! I went from being a bougie girl from big city Los Angeles living a lifestyle of whatever she wanted, whenever she wanted, to nothing, surrounded by a bunch of insects.

Y'all would have been laughing at ya girl. Every time I went outside, I had a fly swatter, killing any bugs near me. I was a mess! Y'all hear me? I was swinging and screaming at the same time. After doing this for a while, I would return to the house. I just couldn't take those bugs. Whenever we had to go somewhere, I made sure I had my fly swatter to swap the bugs, even when getting into the car. This whole thing just made me homesick.

I was missing all of my friends and Mr. Lifeguard too. Man, was I missing Mr. Lifeguard. I cried all the time because I was so miserable. Life started getting a lil rough. My mother enrolled me in Morris High School, where my step dad's niece attended. OMG, this school was NOTHING, and I mean NOTHING, like Dorsey High, nor my friends. Here I was, this city girl who had no filter or fear at this country bumpkin, super slow high school. I stuck out like a sore thumb. However, I started meeting people through my step dad's niece. Everyone thought we looked alike because we were light-skinned, skinny, and cut LOL. She was cool, but not like my friends. My girls from LA were so real. If we had an issue with each other, we confronted it, dealt with it, and moved on staying friends.

Oklahoma was so much different from where I came from. In here, they would talk behind your back and smile in your face. Given my personality, if I overheard someone was a troublemaker who gossiped all the time and they tried to befriend me, I would thank them for their interest in knowing me. Then I would tell them I knew they were a troublemaker/gossiper and that I didn't roll with such people. They hadn't met anyone like me. I was *real*, and they weren't used to that.

The rest of my senior year wasn't that great. I gained a friend outside of my stepfather's niece. My stepfather's nephew, who I became real cool with, had a pretty cool girlfriend to hang out with. However, things started getting rockier in these

Oklahoma streets. My mother and step dad decided to get a divorce. That's right, a divorce! What in the world was going on?

Mr. Lifeguard and I were also on the brink of a horrible breakup. My mother and I weren't getting along because she promised to get me a new car and didn't. I gave away my first car that I bought myself only to move to Oklahoma and have nothing. Oklahoma was a state of broken promises. I saw why people called it the "State of Tears."

I started going through hell. My step dad's nephew and I started being pretty tight. He introduced me to this well-known guy that was a big-time dope dealer. We went to his house a lot and hung out there. My boy cousin (by marriage) and his girlfriend, and sometimes my girl cousin (by marriage) would all go hang out in the country, as they called it LOL. It was the only thing to really do out there. Like, what else could we do? We were in the boonies, the country, with dirt roads and gravel streets.

I remember one day, my boy cousin told me that Mr. G was interested in me. I was like, I got a man, and I don't mess with dope dealers. He was like, "Just take that Nigga's money." I told him I don't roll like that. I don't use people. He then went on to say I should just be cool with him: "You don't have to do anything with him or be his girl or nothing." So I was like, "Okay, we can be cool." My mind was on Mr. Lifeguard. I had never cheated on him. Well, I'd never cheated on anyone I was with. I'm extremely loyal (or so I thought until life started taking its course right before my eyes). I had no idea the things I was going to do to survive in a place where I knew no one.

My mother and I started getting into big fights. I despised that she took me to a state where we knew no one, and instead of returning to Los Angeles, we stayed there struggling and not getting along. Mr. Lifeguard would write to me and send me cards. We could only talk briefly back then because long-distance calls were so costly. That also meant we couldn't speak every day. I stayed depressed, and the only thing that kept me going was hanging out with my cousins by marriage. Which meant we hung out in the country more and more.

I remember I went home to visit for a short min, then went back to Oklahoma only to go to a strange man's house. I was like, when did my mom meet a friend? I hated her friend and couldn't stand this person's kids at the time. Their house was infested with roaches and was nasty. Her friend always wanted to control me. This person didn't like me either because I had no filter. I swear I felt like we moved to a place called "hell". Not only did this move to Oklahoma compromise the lifestyle I was used to, but it also affected my relationship with Mr. Lifeguard. I didn't know how to escape that nasty, infested, roach house. My mom was in survivor-mode; in a place she really didn't know anyone so we wouldn't be out in the street.

I would have my cousin get me and take me to the country where Mr. G hung out with his boys. I started hanging out with Mr. G more often and meeting his mother and family. Many of the women interested in Mr. G did not like me. He would do things for me that he wouldn't do for women he had previously been with, nor give the other women the time of day. They didn't like that. For instance, he allowed me to drive his car.

He spoiled me and just helped me get away from all of the H-E-double L that was going on at the house with my mom. This wasn't healthy because I was in love with Mr. Lifeguard to the point of getting his name tattooed on me before leaving LA. I always wore my promise ring, and felt guilty whenever I looked at my hand. I didn't know how to tell Mr. Lifeguard what was going on in my life because now I had moved into survivor-mode.

All I could think about was that Mr. Lifeguard wasn't ready to take care of anyone yet. I started hearing rumors that Mr. Lifeguard was trying to talk to some of my friends. Everyone who knew me knew they better not talk to Mr. Lifeguard, or we would have problems. This move was becoming more devastating. I started resenting my mother for moving out to Oklahoma and not moving us back after she and my step dad divorced when he got on drugs.

I loved my step dad like he was my father. He would give me anything I wanted; he talked to me, and gave good advice. We would even have food fights at the table sometime. He was fun and a great stepfather. He had taken us to Oklahoma because he had land in the country because he was fully Native American. I don't remember what tribe he belonged to, but his family had reserved land for him. My mother didn't look into what would happen to us in the event of a divorce. Then again, why would she. She thought *this was it…*we *had* to get out. But, enough about that.

Let me finish what I was talking about. One thing about Mr. Lifeguard was that he would tell me the truth if I asked him. So, I asked him if he was trying to talk to some of my home girls. He said, "Yes, I did. I figured you were in Oklahoma doing whatever. But, we both know that after you finish school (college), we are going to be together." I was so hurt because I didn't look at it that way. I cried and cried. I was so hurt. So, I started getting closer to Mr. G. When you start spending time with someone, you start catching some feelings. I felt so bad because Mr. Lifeguard felt like my soulmate, and I thought nothing could come between us. I was in the middle of two lovers and felt so bad about being with Mr. G.

Mr. G would ask me about Mr. Lifeguard, and I was honest about my feelings for him. Yet, Mr. G was not giving up. By this time, he had met my mother. He started coming to pick me up from the house because I hated being there. I eventually started to spend the night at Mr. G's mother's house because me and his older sister and little sister became really cool. My mom didn't know that Mr. G and I liked one another. Things started getting bad at the nasty house with roaches. It wasn't looking good for me. I didn't know what to do. The love of my life, Mr. Lifeguard, and I's relationship started getting rocky too. I started lying to him because I didn't want him to find out about Mr. G, and I didn't want Mr. G to know that Mr. Lifeguard and I were still together and planned on getting married.

Then one day, a choice was made for me. My mama's friend with the nasty house threw me under the bus. Mr. Lifeguard had asked me for the telephone number of the house I was staying at. I gave it to him, not knowing "nasty friend house" was going to answer the phone and tell Mr. Lifeguard where I was at. Not only did Mr. Nasty tell Mr. Lifeguard where I was, but he gave him the dang number. OMG!!! What a mess he made for me. Mr. G talked to Mr. Lifeguard, and chile let me tell you; it was not pretty.

Mr. Lifeguard broke up with me, and Mr. G was ready to hit me over the head with a beer bottle. It was chaotic at Mr. G's mom's house. It took everyone to hold him from hitting me with that beer bottle he had in his hand. I saw hurt in his eyes. I didn't realize that Mr. G had fallen in love with me. Mr. Lifeguard was so hurt he stopped talking to me. Mr. G and I talked it out, but forgiving me took a long time. We kept working it out and breaking up. I was confused and hurt, and I couldn't believe that Nasty made me lose the most important thing to me: the man of my life and dreams, my soulmate, my love, my best friend, my Clyde. All because I was trying to survive and ended up with two men I cared deeply about.

Mr. Lifeguard never forgave me; not for years and years later. Mr. G, on the other hand, we went back and forth for a while. He was so angry at me as well. However, we were able to manage to work it out. I ended up living in the dope house with Mr. G. The place where all the dope heads would come at all hours of the night. I had to tell Mr. G to tell them I had school in the morning and to stop coming by in the wee hours of the night. I was so annoyed, but I had nowhere else to live. Mr. G let me drive one of his cars to school every morning. Man, I had so much going on in my life I almost didn't graduate high school. Mr. G and I had a love for each other, but it was so dysfunctional. After what had happened with Mr. Lifeguard, he didn't really trust me anymore, even though he loved me.

I started hanging out with his sister every weekend, and she would make this drink. It was so good. It was Gin and Hawaiian punch. Man, that drink was so bomb. So much so that I started asking Mr. G's sister if we were hanging out on the weekends cause I wanted some of that Gin and Hawaiian Punch. I didn't realize I was starting to get addicted to it until one day, Mr. G's sister said, "Are you becoming an alcoholic?" Man, that triggered something in me and reminded me of my father's addictions. So, I stopped immediately. However, I started smoking weed and cigarettes to keep myself high LOL.

After a while, I stopped smoking weed but still hung out in the country where everyone would hang out. We would meet up in the county, then go to this place called "The Hut" occasionally. One night, we went to the hut and a few people had got into it and started shooting. I was like, *wait...they shoot out here?* Like we in the country! A bullet almost hit me, but I wasn't scared. Back in the day in LA when Dorsey (bloods) played Crenshaw (crips), we expected shootouts (and you better have your running shoes on)! LOL. We had a lot of fun times in the country at The Hut.

I remember me and Mr. G's older sister and one of her friends went out one night. On our way back, Mr. G's older sister's friend and I were riding in the back seat. I don't remember how we started beefing, but she kept calling me out of my name and I realized she wasn't playing. Now, mind you, she and I were in the back seat of a moving vehicle. Mr. G's sister was driving the car and was like, "Hey, yall chill." She kept calling me a "B-word" after I told her I wasn't her "B". She kept on until I stopped talking, started punching her in the face, and ended up on top of her. I was beating that tail.

Now, she was shorter than me, so I was trying to prevent her feet from getting under. However, she managed to do that, and started kicking me in my chest. Now by this time, Mr. G's sister was like, "Hey y'all, there are cops behind us!" She was getting the best of me with her feet under me. I had never, and I mean never, lost a fight (I once went to a girl's house, knocked on her door, and whooped her butt without fear. She was shorter than me, which gave her an advantage).

Now, we fought for a bit in the back of the car. We pulled over, but she didn't want to fight me then. My chest was hurting from her kicking it really hard. I can't remember if we dropped the girl off or what. I just remember going to the ER to get a chest X-ray. When I looked up, this chick had gotten into the hospital and started fighting me while I was lying on the bed. I was like, "This is my karma." Thankfully, the staff got her out of the hospital.

About a couple of weeks later, Mr. G's older sister's friend fought with this young lady who stripped her of her clothes (outside at a party, in front of everyone who went there on the weekends). She got her butt beat. It was a fight with embarrassment. Could you imagine fighting with someone and getting your clothes ripped off you? God got her for me, and I wasn't even saved yet.

When I graduated from high school, Mr. Lifeguard and I were no longer together; and, Mr. G and I were no longer together. Neither of them could really forgive me for what had happened. I was living with my mother now that she left Nasty alone and got her own place in the city. Mr. G and I stayed friends because he would come by the house from time to time to see my mother. He was really cool with my mom and would stop by to see if we needed anything (even when I wasn't home). He used to call her "E Mama."

In the meantime, I started to get around different areas and meet new people. I still hated Oklahoma but I met this guy named Mr. T. He was cool. We got along very well, but he knew about Mr. Lifeguard. Anyone who met me knew about Mr. Lifeguard because I had gotten a tattoo with his name on my arm. Mr. T and I had a cool relationship, but he was *crazy*. He would let me drive his car when he went to work. I remember staying with him sometimes and cooking dinner for him. We had become really close. As I told you, I don't lie, and sometimes being too honest got me into some crazy positions.

Our town was so small that everyone knew each other or someone who knew them. So, I volunteered to tell him that Mr. G had been by my house and picked me up, and I went to his mother's house to hang out. Even though Mr. G and I weren't dating, I still would visit his mom and siblings. I wanted to make sure no one else told him but me. Now when I told him this, we were on the phone. We talked for a little bit and hung up. He called me back and said he was coming to see me. I was like, "Cool, c'mon." He was cool with my mother as well. Now, mind you, ALL of these men were three to five years older than me.

Anywho, Mr. T came to the house, and we went into my room to talk. Do you know this nut pulled a gun on me and told me if I ever cheated on him, he would kill me? I didn't flinch. He looked at me and said, "You are as crazy as me." Then he put the gun down. My mother was in the other room and had no idea what was happening. Like y'all, I can't make this up. What I didn't know was that Mr. T wanted to marry me. I was still feisty then, with a mouth out of this world and a bad temper. I was young but not dumb. When he told me he wanted to marry me, I told him I was too young to think about getting married. We ended up fading apart. Mr. T was cool though.

Oklahoma was getting crazy, and I still hated being there. A few years after I graduated from high school. I just couldn't take it anymore and went back home to Los Angeles and stayed with my best friend DeeDee. DeeDee and I went all the way back to seventh grade. A group of us hung out, ten of us to be exact. She and I were the two who had long hair, pretty faces, and no body but a booty-bump LMBO. Everyone else's body was shapely. Wait a minute; I forgot one other person, Ms. Robins; she had long hair too.

Ms. Robins was funny as heck when it came to her hair. Like DeeDee and I, she wouldn't let anybody touch or be in her hair. However, Ms. Robins took not touching her hair to a whole other level. She had us rolling on the floor. She would fight her boyfriend for touching or pulling her hair. Heck, she would fight anyone who touched her hair. Now don't get me wrong, Ms. Robin's hair was always on point with the latest style. DeeDee and I would check someone for touching our hair; go off on them, and give them a look, but we didn't fight anyone about it. We were one of those groups where everyone may not like each other, but no one better mess with anyone in the group because they would have to deal with all of us.

DeeDee and I were the closest. She and I became really close, especially after discovering that her mom and my dad went to my grandfather's church (he was a well-known bishop in the Church of God in Christ Arena). His name was Bishop Emanuel Wilson. They still mention his name till this day during convocation. Anywho, let me get back to the story.

I came home to visit for a few months hoping that Mr. Lifeguard and I could talk and work it out. I saw him, and we made love, but he just couldn't forgive me. He was so hurt, though I tried to explain that I had to do what I did. My mother and I weren't getting along, and I felt like I had no choice. We talked about it, but Mr. Lifeguard just wasn't having it. In the meantime, My girl Angel introduced me to her boyfriend's friend named Mr. A. Angel, and I had been friends for a long time, and we had also been with our boyfriends for a few years. I met Angel back in the day (I think, at a ditch party or summer school). However, we hit it off well when we met and became cool friends.

I remember we went on a double date, and the guys took us to Hamburger Hamlet (a very upscale restaurant in Los Angeles). Y'all about to crack up laughing at me! So, we were all sitting at the table and could see people enter the door. When this famous guy was about to walk by our table, I shouted loudly, "Hey y'all, there goes Al Green." Y'all, he looked at me so crazy; like he wanted to cuss me out! Then Angel said, "Girl, that's one of the Isley Brothers!" They laughed at me so hard. When he walked back by the table, I was so embarrassed. Everyone at the table just laughed at me. Woooh, chile that was a funny moment.

Anywho, Mr. A and I got along really well. He and his brother would always come by DeeDee's house on 108th and Crenshaw to see me and hang out quite often. Mr. A and his brother lived literally down the street from Dee. I would walk down to his house and hang out with his family and friends. He and I ended up having a sexual relationship, and I started liking him. Yet, I was still in love with Mr. Lifeguard, hoping we would get over what had happened while I was in Oklahoma.

I was hurt and traumatized so much that I came back home acting wild. I ended up getting pregnant and didn't even know it until I returned to Oklahoma. I was still going out and dancing and getting into clubs. I was too young to be allowed inside, but I was pretty and knew how to talk, so guys would let me in but wouldn't allow me to drink, which I was okay with. I didn't drink anyway. I was the designated driver and loved dancing so much that I could hear music in my head without any song playing and would just be dancing.

After a while, I remembered I needed to take a pregnancy test because my cycle had not started. I went down to get a pregnancy test and found out I was 3 months pregnant. I really didn't know what to do, but I knew I wasn't getting another abortion. That was an experience I didn't want to go through again. So I called Mr. A to let him know that I was pregnant and would keep it. He told me that if I kept the baby, he would kill me. I told him, "If you can find me, then come and do it." Well, I discovered that Mr. A and I had a mutual friend that knew his fiancé. Yes, fiancé. Now, remember that my so-called friend had hooked me up with Mr. A, and not one time did she tell me that he was engaged to anyone—and neither did he. Our mutual friend told me his fiancé had found out I was pregnant. It now made sense why he was so furious about me keeping the baby.

Chapter 4:

SISTER FAITHFUL

So, I'm in Oklahoma, pregnant, and don't know what to do. My brother calls me and tells me not to have the baby cause it will ruin my chances of being a model and mess up my life. *Shoot!* My brother had paid the abortion clinic for me to get rid of the baby, and he was upset because I didn't show up. His dad called me, asking me not to have this baby. I remember going to church and being so torn because I didn't want to get another abortion. That experience really traumatized me.

Madea called me up to the front to pray for me and told me God would make sure we wouldn't want for nothing. I chose to keep the baby. I was so hurt, mad, and didn't know what to do. But I decided to keep my baby despite the odds. And guess what? That didn't ruin my modeling career. Shoot, moving to Oklahoma did. My dream just shattered. As I went along with my pregnancy. I still lived life. I still went out, pregnant and all. I still had fun with the friends I met at the Higher Dimension youth ministry called "The Firehouse" back in the day. By this time, I started finding my way around Oklahoma: from Morris,

Oklahoma all the way to Tulsa, which was more of the city part of Oklahoma (still country as heck though). I was happily pregnant with a baby girl. I was living with my mom and Mr. S. His house was spooky. In my room, I would feel someone getting into the bed and touching me occasionally. I told my mother about it and asked her if someone had died in that room because it was freaky.

I remember telling Madea I felt something kept getting into the bed with me, and I could even feel that thing touching me. She told me to ask what it wanted. I was like, *what*???? Ain't no way I'm about to ask this thing nothing. Instead, I started telling it to leave me alone and go somewhere. I even remember seeing a gray smoke-looking cloud with red eyes in that room.

Now here I am, just saved, and started seeing this stuff. I'm like, "Okay, this is a bit too much for me Lord." I would do anything to stay away from the house—especially for my Princess. One of my friends had introduced me to their cousin that worked at Shoney's restaurant, and he gave me a job there while I was pregnant. Let's call him "Mr. Black." We became really cool, and he would look out for me. He would take me home from work and sometimes come and get me because I was pregnant and didn't have a car. I thought this was so nice of him. We would hang out from time to time, and I remember his mother was a Pastor at a church. She wasn't too fond of me, but Mr. Black told me not to mind her.

We would climb this ladder going up into the ceiling, which was where his room was. It's like he had turned the attic into his bedroom. I thought he was cool because he never tried to get fresh with me. He had become a cool friend who always wore these dark black shades, drove a black BMW, and always wore black. I had to ask him if black was his favorite color, and he said yes. He was cool and funny, which was what I needed. I was pregnant, and in a place I really disliked. But, I was trying to make the best out of it, so I found myself going everywhere, pregnant and all.

The baby slowed me down a little, but I still went wherever I wanted. I remember when it was time to give birth. My mother didn't think I was ready to have her because it was my first baby. I remember having contractions, and man, did it hurt. They had my butt in tears. Like, I don't wish that kind of pain on anyone. The contractions were getting closer and closer, but my mother didn't think I was ready to go to the hospital. I remember calling Madea, and she talked to me for a minute. While we were speaking, I would tell her every time I was having a contraction. I remember asking her to tell my mother that I needed to go to the hospital. My mother didn't want to listen because she was in labor for a long time with her first baby. My mom still wouldn't take me to the hospital until Madea had me tell her that maybe God wasn't allowing me to be in labor that long. I then begged my mother to take me to the hospital.

So with an attitude, my mother finally got dressed and took me. The man that drove to the hospital was hitting all the bumps in the road. So, we finally pulled up to Hillcrest Hospital through the ER. They put me in a wheelchair, and took me up to the area where women had their children to check me to see how much I had dilated. Sure enough, I had dilated to a 6, I believe. They admitted me, and put all the monitors on me so they could keep track of my contractions to see how soon they were coming.

Boy, let me tell you, those doggone contractions made you want to punch someone cause they hurt like a mug and were so close together. Then it was time! My Princess was ready to come out. The miracle I experienced was when I had to push her out. I screamed so loud, crying, because the pain was no joke. My mother was fussing at me, telling me, "Girl, hush all that hollering and just push."

I remember something taking over my body, and I no longer felt the pain while pushing her out. I literally felt the peace of God come all over me and take over after that first push. I will never forget it. That was the second encounter I had with the Holy Spirit. I can't even explain it to you. I hollered. My mother yelled at me and told me to hush and push while she had one of my legs, and immediately I felt the Holy Spirit take over my entire body and help me push my Princess. I was only in labor for four hours total before she was born. Her little fat butt was big. She was almost eight pounds and looked like an Indian baby. I wouldn't allow them to take her out of my room because I had a dream that someone had switched babies on me. I made sure she was always in my sight.

Now, this little girl was bossy while she was a newborn. I remember she just would not stop crying; I fed her and changed her diaper and all. Nothing I did would get her to be quiet. I remember calling Madea saying, "She won't stop crying. I did everything, and nothing is working." So Madea said to me, "Do you have lights on?" I said, "No, just a small light over her bed." Madea told me to turn it off. I turned that light off, and do you know she shut up immediately!? She didn't and still doesn't like the light on when she goes to sleep today. Just *bossy*.

Other than that, Princess was a good baby. My mom would call her "Baby on wheels" cause she would go everywhere I went. At this time, I had started really going to church and dedicating my life to Christ fully. I had become a regular at The Apostle Ministry. That was the name of Madea's church. It was a very small storefront church with about twenty-five to thirty members. Well, it looked like that mainly because everyone had kids which made it look like many people.

I remember taking my baby to church, and Madea told me not to let anyone breathe on my baby or touch her. And if the baby started hollering when someone was around, I shouldn't allow them to touch her. Madea also told me not to let just *anybody* hold my baby nor make her go anywhere she didn't want to go. So, I made sure I kept her close to me. I didn't allow this to stop me from going to church. I was going to church no matter what to enjoy the presence of God.

Some of the members of my church started calling me "Sister Faithful" because I didn't miss church. I ensured I was at church, whether it rained or snowed, or even if I had to catch a bus. I was going to be in the presence of God. Church was cool to me. The name of the church was intriguing to me as well. It was called The Apostleship Ministries. We would see demons talk and cast them out. People purged, doing flips in the Spirit while someone was holding each arm. It was powerful yet theatrical to me. You could feel the power of God. It was electrifying!

Don't let me forget about those white sheets tied around someone to help hold them, the buckets for someone to throw up in, and rolls of paper towels to get what didn't make it to the trash. Whatever you came to church with, it was guaranteed that you wouldn't leave with it. To watch Madea operate in the Spirit, you knew it was God. You could see the power of God on her and moving through her. So, of course, I would run to the church doors every time they opened, no matter how long we would be in church. Sometimes we would be in church until eleven at night while God was having His way. My mother didn't like that I spent a lot of time there or at Madea's house. I would invite her to church, but she wouldn't come with me.

My mother and I weren't getting along because she had talked about Madea so badly. I was afraid of my mother getting in trouble with God. I had a high level of respect for Madea. She made us study for ourselves. Madea would always say, "As soon as you see me stop following God, don't you follow me." She taught us about the lost books of the Bible and told us to go by them. The title was *The Lost Books*. She was a prophet who made us go to the library and learn about each apostle's character and personality. We would have to tell her what we learned and which one of the Apostles we saw ourselves in, personality-wise. She made us study the book of Acts. I was so hungry to learn more about God and why we had to study this particular book. I was twenty-one, and thirsty for more of God and what He wanted to give me through Madea.

Madea would sit me down and tell me I needed to forgive my mother and that it wasn't her fault. Yet my mother kept talking about this woman of God, and I was sick of it. This lady showed me love that I really wasn't getting from my mother. You have to remember, I was still angry and bitter from the move to the broken promises my mother made—just bitter and angry.

To top it all off, when my mother and I argued, she always brought up Madea. I had gotten tired of my mother talking about the woman of God. So one day, I told her to stop doing that before she got in trouble with God. My mother said, "Well, tell her to come and get you then." I went to my room crying, wishing Madea would come and get me. I was just fed up.

One day, not too long after my mother and I had argued about Madea, I visited her. My mom called me and started arguing over the phone. Do you know she packed up all my things, somehow got Madea's address, and dropped all my belongings on her front porch? She then called me, asked to speak to Madea, and told her, "Huh, you can have her. Her things are on your front porch." I looked out the window and saw Mr. Walls walking away from setting my things on the porch…

Now somehow, my mother was cool with all the guys I dated. This guy I had dated, Mr. Wall, had come into town to visit me while I lived in Oklahoma. I really liked Mr. Wall and wish I had chosen him. He was a man that loved God and accepted my child. Even though he looked soft, he was all man. I wished I could've met him in my thirties and not my immature twenties. Anywho, my mother convinced him to pack up all my things in her house and drive with her to Madea's. She had him put all my stuff on the front porch when they arrived. I thought, *"Really, Mr. Walls! You Love me???"*

Mr. Walls would do anything for me. He pursued me and did what he could to show me he loved me. He was willing to move to Oklahoma with me. However, my butt was too blind to see what was good for me. He was a good man and fine. That's why I couldn't believe it was him I saw putting my boxes on the porch. I guess that was his way of saying he was tired of me telling him no. I was too young and too caught up with Mr. Lifeguard to see anyone else, even though we weren't together anymore.

We were in another state, away from my friends. I couldn't call and tell them what I was going through. I was so embarrassed. What was going through my mind about my mom was, "Here she goes again, putting me off on someone else." See, my mom didn't know that outside of Madea being a pastor, she was a foster mother. Madea would get all the kids no one wanted. She was well-known in the foster care community. Madea had an anointing for children. She was always saying, "If you watch how the kids act, you will know how the adults are." Madea would tell us all the time that she rather dealt with kids than adults. LOL. I think this is why she kept her future covered.

I remember sitting on her couch in the living room with the plastic on it. Madea had a vintage type of furniture with a lot of what they called back in the South, "wood knots on the wall of angels." Speaking of Angels, that's when I started having encounters with Angels. The Angels would come into the room, and I wouldn't look at them because I was too scared to. I remember telling Madea, "Can you tell the angels to leave me alone?" They would touch me because I thought I felt something like a peaceful presence. I was like Madea, "Ummera, can you tell the angels to leave me alone, please?" LOL. This was a little different for me. God was changing a lot of things about me.

By this time, I remember going to church, and Madea said to me, "Wonder if God wants you to come out of your pants and just wear dresses?" I responded I would just wear dresses. I had such a zeal for God. The Bible was cool to read. It was like a soap opera to me. There was a lot of drama in the Bible, and I found it very interesting to read; it gave me a love for Jesus. I was saved but still had a boldness.

No one better not talk about my Jesus cause we were going to fight. I didn't care who you were. You better not talk about my pastor or my Jesus, or it was going to be on and cracking. I guess Jesus loved me too. I remember one day at service, it was powerful, and I was slain in the Spirit for two hours. I woke up speaking in tongues. Once I completely came to myself, I got up and stood in the back of the church in between two individuals. Madea preached, and out of nowhere, she said, "You." During this time, I'm looking to my left and right, like, *who is she talking to?* She said, "*You*—the one who was looking at everybody else. I'm talking to *you*." I said, "Who me??" She said, "Yea, YOU. I am talking to YOU!"

All she kept saying was, "I don't know why..I don't know why He chose you, but God chose you to do *work*. God put something down in you that is very special." And she kept repeating herself: "I don't know why He chose you, but He chose you to do work." Now mind you, I wasn't familiar with any of this. I was like, "What kind of work does God have for me to do??" She never went into detail about what work God had put in me. No one told me my suffering was contingent upon the work God had put in me to do.

And let me tell you, my life couldn't get any worse. At least, I thought it couldn't. I remember living with Madea, and I felt like I was dying. I had told her that I felt like my hair was falling out. She would look at me and say, "Do you realize you keep talking about dying?" She wasn't sure what was going on with me. She told me I needed to get my health checked and go to a shelter with my baby. I could get an apartment within two weeks of living in a shelter. So, myself and another sister from the church, ended up going to the same shelter. We were so on fire for the Lord. They would call my room "the sanctuary" because we were recruiting people to God and bringing them to Christ. We also brought a few people to church as well. We wanted to make sure that everyone we came in contact with had an opportunity to know the Lord. We had NO shame!! We felt God had sent us to the shelter to work and bring souls to Christ. We did this for two weeks until my apartment became available.

By then, I was barely making it. I wasn't working and was just getting AFDC and paper food stamps. I paid tithes on my AFDC money and my FOOD STAMPS. If I'd found a dime on the ground, I would tithe a penny. They made fun of me in church for doing so. Y'all just don't know. I was sooo grateful for the little things God would do for me.

I finally moved into my apartment, not knowing that this place was rat-infested. Rats were on the stove and in the cabinets. Man, it gives me the chills even thinking about it now. I was determined not to live in that nasty, infested, rat hole. When I tell you God was humbling a sista, I'm talking about breaking pride off me. I wouldn't have experienced any of this in LA. I knew too many people that would have helped me, especially if I were with a child.

During my pregnancy with my Princess, I stayed with my cousin's girlfriend's family. Y'all know, the one that brought me to Christ? I also stayed with another family that my mom and I met attending Higher Dimension in Tulsa, OK. Then, I ended up back with my mother right before I was due to have my Princess.

I left that apartment quickly, but God allowed me to find another one next to one of my friends' cousins. This is when I had to start cooking. When I was just a child, I watched my mother in the kitchen. She taught me how to cook eggs, smother steak, potatoes, and pork chops (but I didn't like pork chops).

I had a child now and had to learn how to cook. It was hard to think about what I was going to cook. I was poor and struggling. One month I didn't have any food or personal hygiene items, and didn't have the money to buy them. Then God told me to start preparing a meal as though I had groceries. I obeyed the voice and started doing that. Shortly after, I heard a knock at the door, and it was Sista K. I was in shock. She didn't just have one or two bags, she had bags of food and personal items I needed as well. I just cried and cried. I couldn't believe that God would do that for me. Send someone to my house that I don't talk to. Someone I only spoke to at church. I was so grateful. My heart was so full of gratitude.

God had worked so many of these miracles in my life. I was grateful to Him and what He was doing in my life and I became very dedicated to the ministry even though I still didn't have a job. I was still on food stamps and AFDC. However, God made a way for me to go home to LA to visit. By this time, my Princess was old enough for me to travel with her, and I hadn't spoken with her father since he threatened to kill me if I had her. I flew to Los Angeles to see my Dad/Stepmom, whom I stayed with.

Upon my arrival, I decided to stop by Mr. A's house since I remembered where he lived, so he could see my Princess for the first time. I asked my ride to take me there, and they agreed too. We drove to Mr. C's house. I walked up to the door, knocked, then rang the doorbell of the apartment. Mr. A opened up the door. He looked at me as if he saw a ghost. He gave me a long glare and let us into the house. That was the first time he saw my Princess. On this day, we discussed what happened and began a friendship.

I stayed over at Mr. A's house just for a short bit. I then went to my dad's house since he was the reason I visited LA. I was excited to see my dad because I hadn't seen him in a long time, and I had missed him. I thought it was nice of my stepmom to get me a summer job working in her building, making some decent money. The only issue I ran into was who would watch my Princess? My dad was working at the time as well. Hmm, who could I trust? Mr. Lifeguard's mother, maybe? I called Mr. Lifeguard to tell him I was in town. We talked on the phone, and then he came over to my dad's house to visit. He and my Princess played, and he and my dad chopped it up for a bit. Then he left.

As he was leaving, I asked him whether his mom would watch my Princess for me since she had a daycare. She was the only person I would trust with my Princess. Mr. Lifeguard said, "Why don't you go by and ask her yourself. " I said okay, and that I would. I don't remember who let me use their car. However, I drove by his mom's house. We sat and talked for a bit. I asked if she would watch Princess for me, and she said yes. I was so ever grateful for that. *This* started something: Mr. Lifeguard's mom looked at Princess, and told Mr. Lifeguard that Princess was his. He didn't like that too much. See, Mr. Lifeguard had a huge EGO and was upset because I had told him Princess was Mr. A's daughter. So in his words, he replied, "Let that thug take care of him."

To be honest, I wasn't sure, but it seemed that neither of them wanted to do a blood test. Even though Mr. A and I were developing a friendship, it was a little rough at the beginning. He wasn't sure if my Princess was his or not. Whenever I asked him when he would tell his family about my Princess, he would just put me off. I would then go off on him. I asked for a blood test and even offered to pay for it. He refused! Princess started favoring Mr. A's mom. Truth be told, my Princess looked more like me and especially my dad. She had hands and feet like Mr. Lifeguard but resembled Mr. A's mom. Crazy huh? I know.

Mr. A and I never dated. However, he taught me a lot about men. We were so close that whenever I came down to bring Princess to visit, he would call one woman, and she would think she was the only one he was messing with and hang up. He would say, "Watch this," then call another female and run a game on her. This is one of the reasons why we just became really cool. I saw how he was, and he knew I wasn't having that. I was saved but not dumb—at least not with him.

I would talk to Madea about him, Mr. Lifeguard, and my overall life, asking for some kind of guidance. We didn't talk that much as I was still learning her as a pastor. I kept to myself a lot because I wasn't that open to people after what I'd experienced. I didn't really know Madea, but she was easy to talk to whenever I visited her house. This brought me closer to her and allowed me to trust her more.

Chapter 5:

THE JOURNEY

L ife started getting interesting. I didn't know Madea that well to understand that when she said certain things or asked a question, she might be trying to get your attention. This was her way of using wisdom. She didn't believe in getting in the middle of a domestic situation because God isn't the author of confusion. As I became more dedicated to the ministry, I better understood who Madea and the assistant pastor were.

Mind you, at this point, I had only been saved for about two years and was still a little prejudiced. I didn't care for white people that much then, but through my process of salvation, I learned to be cordial with them and forgive those I had racist encounters with in junior high school. You see, I needed a job, and the assistant pastor needed a little help cleaning her house. So, I signed up through DHS to keep them from taking my assistance away. Back in the day, you had to work to keep your AFDC coming in monthly. The assistant pastor was caucasian but was married to a black man who happened to be Madea's son. I was around them quite often. While I was working for the assistant pastor, she told me stories of how a couple of brothers killed themselves because of women. She would tell me many things about her family and sons to get a conversation going.

The assistant pastor had a couple of sons. The three older ones were caucasian, and the youngest was biracial. One just so happened to be fond of me. We became cool, but I had no idea he liked me like that. I often saw him at his mother's house and at church–The Apostleship Ministries. The church was a small storefront; one with few members, but the power of God would move powerfully during service. Her oldest son was like me. He was cool, but I still wasn't that fond of Caucasian people. God hadn't fully delivered me yet. Especially not to marry them.

Even though I was saved and sanctified, I was very depressed. My mother and I weren't speaking, and I wasn't talking to my brother or sister either. But the one that brought me the most pain was my sister because I loved her deeply. In addition to that, I was no longer with the man I was still in love with—Mr. Lifeguard. However, we spoke from time to time. I was just a natural mess. I lost my confidence and no longer thought I was pretty. I sure wasn't expecting my life to look like this: a baby on welfare and food stamps. This is not what I dreamed my life would be like and it shattered my confidence.

The assistant pastor's oldest son started to like me. I wasn't even attracted to him like that. He was fun and funny sometimes and eased my mind by making me laugh when I was down. He tried to have a little soul. I would hang out with him but didn't expect anything to come out of it. We were around the same age, and it was just something to do. I can't even believe that I started liking him a little bit. The more we hung out, the more I discovered who he was. He was charming, would buy me roses, and say the sweetest things. Little did I know his bloodline was so dark. He had a bad temper and was suicidal. I had to take the gun out of his hand because he was trying to commit suicide. I was like, *heck nah*! I had a wake-up call and told him I didn't see him in any other light except as a friend. I just couldn't see myself dealing with anything like that. He even had the nerve to ask me to marry him. I said NO!! I was thinking, "How bad off am I?" What made me even entertain him like that?

When his mother, the assistant pastor, found out that I turned down her son asking me to marry me, she told me if he committed suicide because of the rejection, something would happen to my children. This was a bloodline curse in the assistant pastor's family. She had two brothers kill themself because of a woman. I was like, *what*??? I cried to the Lord because I didn't understand why I had to marry him. I was so afraid because I didn't want to experience the pain of losing another child. Having an abortion was traumatizing enough. So I ended up agreeing to marry him. I remember Madea kept asking if I was sure. She asked me a couple of times, and I said yes. I didn't know her well enough then to tell her I didn't want to marry him and that I was just doing it because I didn't want anything to happen to my children as the assistant pastor mentioned. I didn't know about prayer on that level.

OMG, y'all do not understand that that was the decision from hell, *literally*. I had previously had some encounters with the supernatural, but when I married him, I started encountering demons. I remember seeing things in all black, with hoods on their heads, while I was laying in bed with the lights out; my eyes were open. I just started praying and pleading for the blood of Jesus over me. It went away. I would see this warlock often. I didn't know what it was until I asked Madea. After that, all this stuff about him started being revealed to me. I found out that he was a con artist. One day he almost had me put in jail. He had given me a check to cash and said he earned it from cutting grass. He would cut grass to make money, so I didn't think much of it. I went to cash the check and found out he had forged the signature on the check. Are you kidding me right now??? Thank the Lord for His grace and covering power. The check-cashing place kept the check and let me go. He did this so much that he got caught and ended up in jail. After the incident with the last check, I felt like I was living in a nightmare I wanted to wake up from.

This was a marriage from hell. My life had just gotten worse. I hadn't met his father's side of the family, who lived in Wynnewood, Oklahoma. This boy told them that I was Mexican. Y'all, I can't make this up...well, I found out they were all prejudiced and members of the KKK. Yeah, y'all heard me right. The *KKK*. I was like, "Can this get any worse?? Jesus, what have I gotten myself into?" Ooh, and to top it off, dude was also on drugs! The more I discovered about his family, the more annoyed I became with the assistant pastor. He and I started getting into fistfights because I had a little temper I hadn't been totally delivered from yet. I became really bitter. I remember we fought once, and he wouldn't allow me to get my Princess out of the house. I was so afraid he would do something sexual to her because I didn't trust him. I was screaming and socking him in his face telling him to give me my baby. Every time I tried to run into the house and get her, he would push me, and I would swing at him. We started wrestling on the sidewalk in front of the house. It was around 11 pm.

Someone called the police, who broke it up, but he didnt give me my Princess. I didn't have a phone, and I remember walking down Denver Street in Tulsa at one in the morning. I was praying, crying, and pissed off at the same time. He still had my Princess. Two cars had stopped and asked if I needed a ride or anything. I felt uneasy with the first car, so I didn't get into it. The person in the second car was a gentleman, and I felt a peace in my spirit, so I accepted his help. He took me to his home where I met his wife. They allowed me to use the phone to call my mother and Madea. Madea had someone come and get me and take me to get my Princess. I ended up going to my mother's house that night. I told him he had to leave because that was my house that I got while I was on Section 8. I had so many valuable things in it.

When I returned to my house, someone had robbed me—taken all my things, and tore up most of my high school memories and pictures. I was so hurt and couldn't believe what had happened. They took the furniture my mother gave me and all my teenage memories from Los Angeles that I wanted to keep. I was devastated and felt the need to protect myself and my Princess. At this time, I had put a restraining order on him because I was over it (or so I thought)! I had given him another chance because I thought this was what God had given me, so I decided to make it work. I had sexual relations with him because the Bible said I couldn't deny my husband sex. I didn't want to be the cause of his flesh being weak. I didn't care how much I couldn't stand him; I was dedicated to God and obeying His Word. I didn't want God to be upset with me for disobeying Him. I feared God so much that I didn't want to disappoint or dishonor His Word.

I was catching the bus to church because I didn't have a car and didn't know anyone I could ask to give us a lift. By this time, I had gotten to know Madea a little more. She was my spiritual mother. Sometimes, I would go to her house after church and spend the night there. I was so hungry for God but so miserable at home. I remember getting sick and going to the hospital; the assistant pastor's son stayed with me. OMG…it was such a disaster. I was trying to sleep, and he was sitting next to my hospital bed, when I felt something hit me in my face really hard. I looked up; he was sleeping too. I thought I was tripping. I tried to go back to sleep, and it happened again.

Then I realized that demons were reaching out of his body and hitting me.

I started shaking him to wake up. I was frustrated and told him, "You and your legion of demons move away from me because they keep reaching out of your body to hit me. Your demons keep waking me up." Man, I was so annoyed. When he moved, I was able to sleep and get some rest. Like y'all, I can't make this up. I promise it was like I was having a nightmare with my eyes open. Like, who goes through this type of stuff??? Me!!! I was then released from the hospital because the doctors couldn't find anything wrong with me. Later, I ended up pregnant. I think my Princess was about nine months old. I went through hell being pregnant with my Angel.

All I heard the entire time was *hurry up and have my baby.* I went through a lot of mental abuse with the assistant pastor's son. I was so stressed that I couldn't even finish college and ended up having my Angel during spring break. This was partially my fault because, as a result of what I went through mentally, I didn't even want the baby. Admittedly, I attempted to kill her a few times by having my eldest jump on my stomach, hoping I would lose her. Y'all, it was horrible. I was so poor that someone had given me a box spring to sleep on while pregnant, not the one with the coils but the one with plywood slabs across it. That's all I had to sleep on while pregnant.

To top it off, there was a snake in the house!!! I discovered it one day, and at first, I thought it was a toy snake and was about to pick it up, but something told me, "Do NOT pick that up…" Then I realized it was a real snake. I kept quiet and called the assistant pastor's son to come kill it. This concerned me because it was a baby snake. I knew the momma snake was close by.

We lived in a boxed lil house with no installation but a solid door. I remember one day, I was reading my Word, and someone was literally at the door trying to kick it in. I was as quiet as a mouse, praying and pleading for the blood of Jesus. Whoever it was did not stop kicking that door for what felt like ten to fifteen minutes. They were kicking it so hard that I knew they would get in. The harder they kicked the door, the harder I prayed, calling on the name of Jesus and praying it didn't come open. Whoever it was finally went away.

I was scared out of my wits. I kept saying, "Thank you Jesus, thank you Jesus," while crying. I was seven months pregnant when this happened. Madea would call me often, asking how I felt and if I was home alone. One day I finally asked her, "What's wrong because you keep asking me if I'm okay and alone?" She responded, "You just don't need to be home alone," and didn't volunteer any more information.

It was spring break, and I was home alone. My water broke, and I wasn't sure if that was what was going on or not because my water didn't break with my Princess. Instead, the nurse broke my water. That was the weirdest feeling ever, peeing on myself but having no inclination that I needed to use the restroom LOL. I was like, *what was that*? I was a little OCD, so

I was mad at myself because I peed on my cover while trying to reach the landline phone in this little area in the front they called a room. I was so embarrassed LOL. I called Madea, who told me to call my mother and let her know I was alone and my water broke. My mother picked me up and took me to the hospital. When I arrived, the nurses took me upstairs to the mothers' room. They put the monitor on me and did an ultrasound. The doctor admitted me because he discovered some issues. He told the nurse to induce me because my Angel had the umbilical cord tied around her neck. They had also found blood spots on her spine. During this time, my mother was in the hospital with me.

Let me pause for a moment. Even though my mother and I had some issues, she has always been there for me with all of my children. She saw all the pain in my eyes and all the suffering I went through. I am very grateful for that. My mother did her best with the cards she was dealt.

Back to the story...the assistant pastor's son finally showed up, and I had my Angel after that. She was so small; she weighed four pounds. I couldn't keep her in the room with me due to her medical complication from being born prematurely. My Angel was so little. I had the worst time because she died a couple of times while in the ICU. I cried and stayed beside her crib as long as the nurses allowed me since she was in ICU. I couldn't hold her. I could only touch her little hands, pray, and cry. Looking at her in that condition hurt me so much, not knowing if she would live. After a few days passed, they told me she was having complications with her heart and had to be put on a heart monitor. I was so sad and hurt.

I remember telling Madea what was going on with my Angel. She came up to the hospital to the ICU where my Angel was. My Angel was laying on her stomach. Madea rolled up in her wheelchair and gently touched her from the top of her head to the soles of her feet while praying for healing and said a special prayer under her breath. When she was done, she looked up at me and just smiled. I knew then that my Angel was going to be okay. I hated seeing her like that.

Leaving my Angel in the hospital was so hard, but I had to trust God. I was so hurt that I couldn't take her home with me. She stayed in the hospital for about two weeks or so until the doctors thought she was steady, and her brain and lungs were developed enough for her to come home. You would think this would have brought the assistant pastor's son and me closer. NO!!! It made it worse for my Angel and me. I dealt with so much mental abuse when she came home.

We would argue so much that her heart monitor would go off. Then he would stop arguing with me. It was bad y'all. I remember going to church, and I had my Angel with me, and he tried to snatch her out of my arms. Mind you, she was fragile and still on a heart monitor. I would hold her so tight as he yelled at me, saying, "Give me MY baby..." OMG, he would say that so much as if I had never birthed her. This happened a few times. I had to put him out and get another restraining order because he fought me, then took her and brought her back, saying, "Feed my baby and leave." Not too long after getting a restraining order, he ended up in jail for committing fraud again; this time he got five years. I remember I was a hairline from losing my mind—*but God*. Being married to the assistant pastor's son felt like I married hell. But I was still just trying to obey God's Word and not divorce him.

After he got out of jail, we moved to Wynnewood. Man, we were so poor. We lived in a house with a hole in the roof. Every time it rained, we had to put a bucket in the kitchen to catch the rain so it wouldn't flood. I remember when our lights were cut off, and we used our BBQ grill and light to cook eggs, pancakes, and meat for breakfast. The struggle was real. I had to stretch my money. I still had food stamps, and people gave me money, so I had some cash. I also learned how to mow yards to make money. I would take the riding lawn mower to the store because I didn't have a car to use for picking up groceries. I fed two kids and two adults for only twenty dollars. I would dig in trash cans looking for glasses to drink out of because I couldn't afford glasses. Once, we went to a college trash can where students were leaving their dorms at the end of the semester and found brand-new glasses still in the box. I would soak the glasses and utensils in bleach. Then we moved to Wynnewood in the middle of nowhere.

Man, I thought it was bad when we lived in Tulsa. Whew, it got even worse when we moved to Wynnewood. This is the town the assistant pastor's son and family grew up in. All of their family lived here. Now mind you, I told you that his father's side of the family thought I was Mexican because that's what he told them. Why did he tell them that? Great question! He knew they were prejudiced and didn't want them to know I was African American and Puerto Rican. Oh, baby, when they got the chance to meet me in person...*no bueno* (no good). But because my baby Angel looked more on the Caucasian side, they were more accepting since she didn't look black. She even had big black fluffy curls like her dad. So it was easy for them to accept her.

Now me, on the other hand, when his family realized I wasn't Mexican but Black and Latino, boy...y'all should have seen their faces when I walked through that door with him and my angel. Hahahahaha, that mess was hilarious. Complete silence with a forced hello. I was cracking up on the inside and was like, "I guess this one Nigga, they'll have to learn how to love because if they wanted to see their grandchild, they would have to look at *this* Nigga. It was very difficult for his stepmom to adapt to my angel's hair. See, my angel had very, very silky long hair. One day, the girls had to go to childcare because I was working, and my Angel got lice. Wheeeeew, the Lord knew I was about to cut all her hair off. I used the lice medicine to get them out and that little comb to take out the dead lice, only for her to get it again and again. Finally, I forgot who told me to use mayonnaise in her hair and put grease because lice only stick to dry hair. I applied the grease after washing her hair, and I've never had that problem again.

I was so traumatized by the lice incident I told her step-grandmother to stop washing her hair every night because it removed the grease. I reminded her that although she looked like a Caucasian, she wasn't and needed grease in her hair. We fought about this for a long time, so I told her, "If you can't respect what I'm asking you to do regarding my angel's hair, she won't be coming over there anymore to spend the night." After that, I didn't have any more problems with her washing out the grease in her hair. In fact, she also started applying it to my baby's hair. Now y'all, this is just the issue I had with my step-grandmother.

Y'all, when I first met his one brother that was part of the KKK, he spat in my face cause I was Black, and I remember looking at him laughing, saying, "This is one Nigga you're going to love." Then another time during our divorce, he and his girlfriend took my baby girl, and his girlfriend kept calling my baby the 'Nigga baby.' Y'all, this was so hard for me. I would pray for hours to God, in tears, and read my Word to find comfort. However, the only thing I would find was strength and continuous boldness as I read about the Apostles and the life of Christ and how He handled people when He was being mistreated. I started feeling like a doormat. I was told to be humble cause y'all don't know how many times I wanted to bring that fearless LA girl from the J's out and go off and whoop someone's butt. I was experiencing *Racism 101*.

It didn't make it any better that the assistant pastor would talk about me. She was one of the nastiest people I had ever met. Now, when I was growing up, we had a roach here and there. But that women's house was infested with roaches like that was their hibernation place. Then, she would walk around with flip-flops on, and they were nasty looking cause she would be in her garden with her toenails full of dirt allllll the time!! She was just nasty.

I was so tired of her talking about me, and I'd had enough. One day, we were all at Madea's house, and I couldn't hold it in anymore. On this day, for just a moment, the girl from the streets of LA came out, and I went off. I told her everything I ever wanted to say to her. I was just sick of it. I had realized that she was prejudiced too, even though she had a black husband and a mixed son. She just liked her man, but the rest of us was just Niggers to her. I told her off too. After that, I apologized to Madea for bringing stuff on her cause she already dealt with enough with the church folks. She carried a lot in the spirit. I left and went home.

By now, I was five years into this marriage from hell by paper. The good thing is that we only lived with each other for a year and 6 months in total because he was in jail for fraudulent activities most of the time. Being married to him was not a pleasant experience. I remember one time in church, one of his demons gave me a black eye while I was in the spirit. I didn't even know until Madea said, "Baby, what's wrong with your eye?" I said, "Nothing," and she said, "There's something; you have a black eye." I said maybe I hit myself on my knee while I was in the spirit. She said, "No, I was watching you; no one was near you." She then prayed that whoever did it, should return to their sender. Then, my husband's arm popped out of place immediately. I kid you not. It was one of his liaisons with demons fighting me again. I didn't believe it, but everyone kept saying no one was near me to even hit me. I was like, *are you guys serious?* I had never in my life experienced anything like that. Can you even imagine? This was a marriage straight from Hell. I was saved, prayed daily, and went to church every day of the week except Saturday. However, depending on whose house you were at, a church may break out of nowhere. I didn't understand why I was going through all of this.

Not too long after this happened, Madea, myself and the assistant pastor had gone for a ride in the van, and the subject came up as to why I married the assistant pastor's son. I then told Madea the story of how the assistant pastor told me that if I didn't marry her son, something would happen to my children. Madea looked at me as the assistant pastor claimed God said that I was her son's wife. Madea looked at me, dropped her head, and said, "God ain't told me that."

After that ride, I immediately went to the courthouse to get a divorce. During our divorce, he had gotten a great attorney, and it appeared he would win custody of my Angel. I didn't know where to go, when someone at work told me about this divorce attorney in Pauls Valley that worked out a retainer. I called him, met up with him, and was able to pay him throughout the case. This divorce was so bad. I was crying out to God because he was about to have my Angel, and I wouldn't be able to protect her. I cried and cried, asking God to please not let him take my baby. By sight, it looked as though he was winning. But God had told me to just believe. I didn't have enough money to pay the attorney anymore. It was rough y'all. I just knew he was about to win this case.

Then one day in court, his attorney didn't show up, and my attorney did. On the last court date, I was so afraid. I didn't know what would happen because neither of our attorneys showed up, but not only that, her dad didn't show up for court either. At this point, the judge had granted me full custody and divorce in a court docket. I cried and cried because now, he couldn't take my baby from me. I had gotten a restraining order against him and his father, so no one could take my baby Angel.

A few years after the divorce, I moved in with Madea and became her armor bearer. Madea was a foster parent with few kids but was very wise. She taught me a lot of spiritual things. She was a prophet born with a veil over her face. These prophets are very rare. Living with Madea, I experienced a lot of signs and wonders and angels too. I would also see how the church folks tried to poison her, steal from her, and just saw the true hearts of those that were part of the congregation. A few years later, Madea asked me if I remembered everything she had taught me. I said yes, and started telling her what she had taught me. She looked at me and said, "As long as you remember what I taught you, you will be okay." Not too long after that, Madea told us she was about to go home to the Lord. A week later, she ensured her house was clean, gave us many instructions, and went home to be with the Lord the following day. She visited me in spirit and told me never to give up. This started my journey alone. An unknown life—a life open to deception.

Chapter 6

THE VOICES OF DECEPTION

You would think I would know deceit when it comes. Well, I learned that deception comes in different forms. The enemy uses what's in you against you. See, I believed everything I read in the Bible and lived by it, especially when obeying the prophets and the blessings that came with it. That was until I met Mr. Graham. Mr. Graham was a brother to one of my coworkers at the State School in Pauls Valley, where I once worked. My coworker used to tell me about her brother quite a bit, but I was in my own world. She said she wanted me to meet him, how he looked, and how I would just love him.

Well, during this time, I was moving back and forth from Wynnewood to Tulsa and back to Wynnewood for what seemed like every six months. This was my bipolar behavior because I respected Madea so much that I wouldn't sin in the same city. I was a sinner in the summer, and in the winter, I was a saint LOL. Don't y'all judge me! Y'all know what I'm talking about. I was still trying to figure out this process of salvation and sanctification LOL. Anywho, during this time, I suppose Mr. Ham's sister thought so highly of me that she had this man looking for me so we could meet. How do I know this??? Because when I moved back to Wynnewood from my sinning fun in Tulsa, I had a card on the door of my apartment that I had JUST moved into. I had come home from work with a man named Mr. Ham on my door. I should have known then to run, but I was so curious about this man who was bold enough to leave a card on my door. How did he find me? So, I ended up calling the number on the phone with hesitation. He answered, and I said, "Hello, may I speak to Mr. Ham?" He then stated, "This is he," in his very studious voice, sounding very educated. I then asked him, "How do you know me and how did you find out that I was living back in Wynnewood?" It was creepy yet intriguing at the same time. I was like, "If you're doing all of that just to find me, I guess I can see what you're all about."

So, we hung out a few times and talked a lot on the phone. I had been invited to a prophetic conference and wanted to see if he knew God. I asked him to join me, and he agreed. Okay, that was a brownie point for him LOL, but I was still observing him. We arrived at the church and sat at the back. God was moving during worship. Everyone sat still because we were taught to be quiet while the prophetic flow moved so we didn't disturb and interrupt the spirit. The prophet started prophesying before calling Mr. Ham up to the front. He started talking to him and asking if he was married. Mr. Ham said no. Then the prophet told him God said that the woman in his heart was his wife. Then he asked him if that woman was in the congregation. Then Mr. Ham turned around, looked at me, said yes, she is in here, and pointed at me. I looked at him like, "I just met you; how am I the woman in your heart?"

The prophet asked me to come to the front, and I did. Then he told me that I was his wife. On the inside, I was like, *no, I'm not. I don't even know this man like that.* Even though EVERYTHING in me said don't marry him, I wanted to obey what the Bible said: "obey the prophet, and you shall be established." It was a war against obeying the prophet and listening to my inner man telling me not to do it. Because I was so big on obeying God and making sure I submitted to those that He called prophets, I overrode what I was feeling on the inside. No one taught me that God lives INSIDE of us and gives us all intuitions/gut feelings that come from the Spirit within. That is what we should listen to because that's what bears witness to our confirmation. We don't have to receive a Word from a prophet if it doesn't bear witness to our spirit.

I dreaded marrying him because I didn't feel he was what God had for me. I assumed I was wrong because the prophet said something different, and he was the one that heard from God. The prophet married us. Man, let me tell you. OMG, the hell I went through. So, the woman in his heart was actually a young Caucasian lady he had been dating for a few years and had broken up with. Mr. Ham found me in between their break up. Man, round two of the devil territory was crazy. All of this was for trying not to dishonor God and His word.

When she started coming by the house, he introduced me to her as a friend he had known for a long time. I kept watching and praying. I started discerning that the both of them had a lot more going on than friendship. So, I remember asking him if he used to date her, and he told me the truth. See, after breaking up, she called him to apologize, but he told her he was married. This truth came out later. In my head, I'm like, this is the lady the prophet was referring to when he told him the woman in his heart was his wife. So, now I'm irritated because here I am again in a situation just trying to obey God's Word about "believing the prophet, and you shall be established." I'm like, what kind of establishment was the Bible referring to (because I'm cautious about the different people that call themselves prophets and question the word as well)? I remembered what my godmother Madea told me: "man will mess me up." But, God had told her that HE would teach me. Let me tell you, He taught me what was not of Him through the things I suffered. The more I suffered, the more I sought God and His Word.

She started coming by the house quite often, and he and I started getting into it quite a bit because of her. I remember when we were in the snow, he smothered my face with snow, and I almost stopped breathing. I was mad. I started getting off him, bringing her up. One day, he provoked me to anger, and I threw a shoe at him, and the tip of my heel hit him smack in the middle of his chin. After that, it was history. I ended up moving out, and he divorced me six months later—on my birthday.

I moved back to Tulsa a few years after being divorced and started attending this prophet church in north Tulsa. I really loved the church because they prayed a lot, and prayer was what kept me closer to God. I don't remember how I found out about the church, but I attended for about a year before meeting husband number three. Let's call him Mr. Dub. This church felt like family because the Pastor would always have stuff at his house after church. He was really funny and cool too. His wife was loving at the time and a warrior in the spirit. They were all cool. I felt like I had finally found a church I could call home. I was able to be my spiritual self. I made sure I attended all the time and paid my tithes.

Around this time, I focused on getting closer to God and raising my children. I was regaining my strength in God, seeking Him the way I knew how. I had been committed to church for almost a year now when Mr. Dub appeared. He popped up at church, I guess, after being gone for whatever reason. I would see him and say hello, then go on about my business. He was handsome and quite charming, but he could also see in the spirit, pray his butt off, and beat the rings off a tambourine. However, I had heard that he had been married, was separated, and going through a divorce. I by no means wanted to get caught up in that.

Pastor used to have gatherings at his house almost every Sunday. They would always invite the girls and me over to fellowship. One day, I decided to go, and from there, I was always at the Pastor's house. The pastor and his wife became like family to my girls and me. We had so much fun. It seemed like those who attended the church were comedians too. We used to clown one other but checked on each other too. It was like a little "church gang" because everyone was about *that* life—from the men to the women, but would pray you out of hell in a minute. I loved that about this church. We could be holy and still human. This is where I learned I had the gift of healing in my hands. My hands would be on fire whenever someone around me needed healing. I remember when Mr. B had a headache, I asked if I could lay my hands on him and he said yes. I placed my hands on his head where the headache was. After a few minutes, his headache was gone. God had taken it away. I was in awe of God and how He worked through people. I never knew that gift was in me until then.

I didn't realize Mr. Dub was everything I had written in my Bible about the kind of Godly man I wanted to marry. He knew how to pray and had a strong sense of discernment. His discernment was so on point that if someone walked past him, he could tell what type of spirit they had. He also encouraged me and taught me different things about my gift. In addition, he was a family man. He even knew how to cook and was a hard worker. See, when I wrote what I wanted in a husband, I was speaking from an unbalanced place—what I was led to believe a man of God *should* look like. I wanted to be taught about asking for what I want from a balanced place. I know you're like, *a balanced place?* Yes—a place of asking for a man with spiritual and natural balance. You're probably asking what I mean. Well, everything I had written about what I wanted in a husband was spiritual. I wanted a man that could see in the spirit, pray a demon away, cover me in the Spirit, and have all these spiritual attributes, but I forgot to ask for other things.

Like, a man with a certain type of character, a man with a particular type of mindset, an honest man, a man that was secure within himself, and a man with goals and dreams. A man that I trusted to lead, so I would humbly follow. A man of supernatural faith that also knew when to be practical. These were the qualities I wanted.

Now don't get me wrong, Mr. Dub had some great attributes. He was funny as heck and didn't believe in gender roles. He was good with the kids. I know you're like, what happened to Mr. Bud and me? Well, a few things. First, when Mr. Bud and I got together, he was going through a divorce with his second wife. He had two boys from his first marriage, two boys from his second marriage, and a little girl he raised as his own. Well, during this time, the wife wasn't attending church. Now Mr. Bud had been watching me for a while. I thought he was handsome but still kept my distance until one day…we were all at the Pastor's house having fun like one big family. He looked at me while we were in the kitchen area. He was putting on his shoes and told me, "As soon as my divorce is final, I'm going to marry you." As I looked at him, thinking that sure was a bold statement he had made, he repeated it with a knuckle. "You think I'm playing? I am not playing. I'm going to marry you. Watch…" I was like, "Yeah, yeah, whatever. We'll see."

Not too long after, he found an opportunity to catch me by myself in the pastor man cave/movie room set up like a den. The girls and I spent the night over there. Other kids were at the house where my girls played, and they wanted to spend the night. Mr. Bud started kissing me, and it felt so right. Nice and slow and wooed me right out my draws...LMBO. He got me from the back; after that, it was a wrap. Now the Pastor, being a prophet, knew we were having sex in the den. I felt so convicted. I had been celibate for about two years. I feared what the pastor would say to me. He fussed us out. I took it, apologized, and went on really liking Mr. Bud.

Now, Mr. Bud was the husband I chose to marry out of my own will. It was rough at the beginning because his wife wanted him back. I was new to this church, and I didn't know they had been members here for some time but hadn't been coming for whatever reason. Then one day, she showed up wanting her husband back and asking the pastor to pray for him back home. Mind you, I was sitting in service, sitting next to Mr. Bud while all this was happening. I was like, *what in heaven's name am I in the middle of???* It was so embarrassing.

I didn't want to be the reason someone got a divorce. So, I started talking to him about working it out with his wife. He kept saying he loved her but he was done and wanted to pursue something with me. I felt so bad, but he would talk me out of feeling that way. He and I had started living with each other. Something had happened, and he needed a place to stay. So, I allowed him to stay with the girls and me. Can you imagine how rough it was for me? I felt so conflicted, yet I was falling in love with him.

We had a lot of laughs together until all this stuff started happening at church. Y'all, I promise it felt like a live soap opera. You would never believe the things that took place. The wife started coming to the church crying, wanting him back—it was happening often. Then, this lady they called a prophet, started coming to the church to minister. She called Mr. Bud and his wife up to the front, looked at her (the wife), and told her that Mr. Dub was her husband God had given her while I was sitting there. OMG, y'all, this was so embarrassing. Mr. Bud said, "I don't want to go back." Let's just say I found out a lot about who Mr. Bud was. When I talked to him, he convinced me that he had changed. Mr. Bud was abusive to his wife.

You would have thought I would have known better after everything I had been through. This was an absolute mess, but Mr. Bud would not let me walk away. At this point, I'm shrugging on the inside like, if that's your God-given wife, you need to be with her and find a way to work it out. Mr. Dub was not hearing that. He had convinced me that he was done and that the lady was no longer his wife. I'm like, *but you two have been together for fifteen-plus years, and you're over her just like that? No way!* I struggled with this for a while because I felt bad for messing with a married man and falling in love with him. I cried a lot during this time because I was torn between obeying the Scripture, following my heart, and wondering whether to believe what he was telling me. He was such a powerful man of God that just needed to see a true example of what a real man of God looked like. Mr. Bud was everything I wanted in a man of God. My heart and his charm convinced me to believe that he was done. I stayed with him as he completed his divorce process. Later, we ended up getting married at the courthouse in Dallas.

We didn't have much, but I had a lot of faith. He had three children, and I had two. We wondered what we would do with all of the children because where we were staying wasn't big enough for us all to live. One Sunday, the pastor preached about faith. I acted upon what the pastor had spoken. I was like, *I'm going to try what he said.* I thought, "I have nothing to lose by believing and seeing if it'll come to pass." So, I found a nice house that God directed me to. The owner found favor in me. I didn't have to give a deposit or prove we could pay the rent. The house had an upstairs, downstairs, and a pool in the backyard. All the kids had their own rooms, and we blended together as a family.

We made it work. Mr. Bud was a family man who would help me around the house with the kids, and didn't mind cooking (even though both of us worked). His spiritual eye was so keen he could see right through people and their motives. He was my helper in the spirit. The only thing is that he was more loyal to the pastor than me. So much so that he would get in my face, ready to fight me. It was so unhealthy—it put a strain on our marriage, causing unnecessary arguments. Man, that was *nothing*. The pastor had lost his house, and his family needed a place to stay. Despite our fights about their unhealthy armor-bear relationship, the pastor was good to us. Mr. Bud and I agreed to let the pastor and his family stay with us. Boy, we made the wrong decision. He just took over our home as if it was his house but didn't contribute to the bills. He was loud, left all the lights on, and allowed anyone to come by the house without asking. My house was my sanctuary and peaceful space, but that was all taken away. The pastor started calling me crazy, and I would tell him I was not crazy.

This started after the assistant pastor announced that anyone who felt they were called to preach should come to church on Sunday at 8 am before service started. They would conduct a five minute sermon and would then be told the areas they needed to improve on. I was so happy about this because I knew God had called me to preach and this was an opportunity for me to learn how to do it. The assistant pastor called it, "Preach Preacher, Preach." Y'all don't know, but I was ready and nervous at the same time. Mr. Bud was supportive and helped in this area. That's another great thing about him; he supported me and was helpful when it came to doing the Lord's will.

I was so nervous during my first Preach Preacher, Preach session. God woke me up early that Sunday and gave me a Word. I started realizing that I was a teacher. I'm not sure how well I wrote everything, but I guess I couldn't go wrong with God leading me on what to write and how to write it. So, we showed up a little bit before 8 am and waited for the others that were also participating so we could walk inside the sanctuary together. I was so nervous, but Mr. Dub was very encouraging yet funny at the same time. He kept telling me, "Ohh don't mess up because we are going to talk about you and help you at the same time." He was a clown but told me the truth. Remember, we were a clowns-that-loved-God type of a family LOL.

We started arguing a lot because I was starting to worry too much, still had the street in me, and was tired of running from the situation. On top of that, the pastor kept calling me crazy. I would tell him to stop doing that and projecting onto me by saying that I thought I could preach better than him. Yet, I never said or implied anything of the sort. Like, I'm your lay member that looks up to you and respects you. This was hard because they lived in our house. His accusations were so strong to the point that they started attacking my mind. I remember I was up in our room praying and talking to God. The spirit attacked me so strongly that I called a young lady to pray with me, but it didn't help. As I was praying, Mr. Dub walked in and laid on top of me and started to pray in the spirit, binding, and rebuking as I was pleading the blood of Jesus over my mind, and that thing broke off of me.

We were good for a short while, then Mr. Dub's other baby mama came to town to visit his other baby mamas. I went over to the house and that was the worst mistake I could have ever made. It's like I walked into a grenade meant for me. The eldest baby mama started to get smart like I'm supposed to just sit there? I stood up for myself, and Mr. Dub jumped on her side like I was some random girl at the house. I'm like, *what the hell is going on here?* We argued at the baby mama's house, and I left. Mr. Dub started chasing me, and the LA chick came out. I started running lights, hitting corners, and driving to the house where the pastor and his family were (as well as some guests). I pulled up, ran into the house, grabbed a butcher knife, and waited for him to pull up as the pastor called my name. I went insane briefly because I wasn't hearing anything anyone was saying. I was determined to stab him that night; I was tired and had had enough.

Mr. Dub came into the house looking for me. I yelled, "I'm in the kitchen. Come near me and I'm going to stab you." The pastor in the background heard us struggling over the knife while Mr. Dub was trying to take it out of my hand and cut me. The guest in the house grabbed him, and the pastor stated, "If you touch that girl, I'm calling the police, and you're going to jail." He kept telling him, "You better not," so many times. They held him back while I packed a bag for my girls and me, and we left.

Later, the pastor talked to the two of us. We had a conversation, and he apologized. We then decided to make things work because I really cared about him. I didn't realize how this was affecting my girls. I just know that one of my daughters wasn't having it. My girls would see me cry and come pray with me and over me. They were my strength in so many ways. Things continued to escalate even though we talked. His loyalty to the pastor was an unhealthy one. What made it worse was the pastor didn't see anything wrong with it. Not only did the light bill start becoming outrageously high, it was in *my* name. The pastor had no thought about the lights and never offered to help pay the electric bill (even though not only he and his wife lived with us, but we also accommodated their 3 children, who were about the same age as my daughters). I took care of my two girls and his 3 children too. We had the room, but the water, electric, and gas bills were pretty high. The only bill in my name was the electric bill which was the only bill that wasn't being paid, and it was the highest one. The electric bill was so high I asked Mr. Dub to talk to the pastor to help us pay for it, but Mr. Dub refused. It started to become too much.

After having another bad fight and seeing that he wanted to hit me, I started plotting how I would move out with my girls. God revealed to me that he and the pastor planned to take the furniture. So God started showing me how to move strategically. I heard His voice so clearly, as though He was standing right beside me talking. He told me to get a restraining order against the pastor and Jr. So, when I was home, neither of them would be allowed to come in the house while I was moving. This was because the pastor wouldn't hit me, but he was just as loyal to Jr.

So, God gave me the date and the time to get a moving truck, load the truck (with some help), and even what time to get there. I obeyed and got to the house before them. You should have seen their faces. They were shocked to see me there because they thought I was at work. But let me tell you, when you listen to God's voice, His plans will be ahead of the enemy's plans. When they pulled up to the house, I was almost finished loading the truck. He asked for a few items, and I told him he could have the bed. I had called the police and showed them the restraining order, and they made sure no one came into the house until I was gone.

I moved to my place with my girls and continued living my life. Mr. Dub went back to Kansas to stay with his parents. We separated for a few months and then started talking on the phone. He started apologizing to me and telling me how much he loved me. He was sorry and asked if I would take him back.

Now, Mr. Dub was very good with his hands and computers. He had his insecurities. However, I felt like he could get a certificate in rebuilding computers and start his own business. He was good with taking computers apart and putting them back together again, and he enjoyed it. So, I agreed to take him back if he was willing to go to school, get his computer certificate, and start his own business to build his insecurities. I agreed to pay the rent and find some time for us and our four children (because his daughter had moved back with her mother). So, it was just my two girls and his two boys. He agreed, and I committed to getting a two-bedroom. I bought two bunk beds, one set for the girls and one for the boys. I found a two-bedroom condo for five hundred dollars a month. I had a job, and I'd just gotten a raise, enabling me to pay rent and the bills while he was going to school. This was the agreement we had if he were to come back.

I found a place in a great neighborhood and school district. Then Mr. Dub and the boys came back to live with us, and he started returning to the church. I told him I wasn't going back there. I had found another church to attend. Sure enough, I regretted even taking him back. He came down and never enrolled himself in school, saying, "I'm not doing that." So, I was working while he was just home during the day. I worked right down the street, and things weren't sitting right in my stomach. I would call him during my lunch break to see what he was doing. He started getting nasty with me and started saying, "Bitch stop calling me," and hung up in my face. I'm like, *who is he talking to*? Then, I would come home, and my house didn't feel right. I would smell Bath and Body Works on my pillow, which I didn't wear, and he would say, "I'm smelling stuff."

I came home from work another time and found a bottle of wine in my bathroom. He kept telling me nothing was going on. Then I started noticing the hand towels I kept in the bathroom started getting low, or I would see other colored towels. So, I started refilling the towel rack and counting them and writing the number down on a piece of paper. When I came home, I would count the towels, and it would be a few towels off. Then, I found a damp towel that didn't belong to him or me hanging on my towel rack to dry. There was so much going on. At the time, someone at work was hitting on me and fighting to get my attention. Mr. Dub and I hadn't been intimate in a while. Cheating wasn't my style, so I told him, "Someone is trying to get my attention at work, and I wanted to let you know what's going on." Well, all of this time, I had a prayer partner I was confiding in, and she told me all the signs showed he was cheating on me. Now, I started watching certain things: her movements and his. I don't know what made me start paying attention to these two. But I did, and God started showing me stuff. Even his pastor confirmed it.

He and I got into a huge argument in our room, and one of my daughters yelled, "Leave my mama alone!" He turned the door and swung her against the wall. I heard the voice of God say, "Don't do it, Danyle; start being extra nice." I was like, "*What*? God, are you kidding me!? Did you see what he just did to my baby?" He still said I should be extra nice. I listened because God told me he would leave on his own without a fight. So, I did that and became extremely nice to the point where he became afraid of me and what I may do to him in his sleep. Eventually, he left the house. The only thing about him leaving was that he did my girls and me so dirty.

He took the car and took the electricity out of his name. Then I found out that the bill he told me his pastor was going to pay off ($1200) was never paid. It was a bill I owed because it was my name. I also had just quit my job, so I had no income. I just cried and cried to the Lord and went into prayer. I was angry. I went to God and said, "I will try You at Your Word to see if it's real. I'm going to put it into action." So, I took the Scripture, "Seek ye first the kingdom of God and His righteousness and ALL of these things shall be added unto you." I also took the other Scripture before it that says "How good is it to lay your life down for someone else." I started praying for my abusive husband and everyone I thought wronged me. I asking God to bless them, deliver them, and provide for their every need. Then I found a church home and I started hanging out there.

I had started working for Wilson Leather and the manager there invited me to church; I went, and loved it. This was a few months before all the other stuff started happening at home. I worked there part-time to make some extra money because I knew I would quit my job. I had been on that job for four years; two of those years doing management work and getting paid as a rep. I agreed to do it to get the experience under my belt.

I took over a special project for one of the managers and perfected that. I then started working for HR. I was doing the job tours for everyone that was applying and scheduling testing. So, I was working two jobs out of my paid grade and was never offered a raise. Then a position became available in HR. I applied for it. They wouldn't allow me to apply as a supervisor even though I had supervisors that were requesting my help as they watched my work ethic. Still, I was not able to excel. I realized that certain people were intimidated by my ambition, thinking that I wanted their job. I was just trying to learn the job, excel in the company, and turn it into a career. I realized it wouldn't happen, so I quit my job. Not too long after, things got rough and out of hand at home.

After submitting a divorce, I was finally free from the old pastor's abuse and toxicity. To put the icing on the cake, the person that called themself my prayer partner and who said Jr. was cheating on me, was actually the one cheating with him. I was so devastated and hurt; so much that I wished for her death. Yeah, *death*. I meant every bit of it. I used to take care of her, pray for her, and would've given her my last dime if I had it. Yes, I was traumatized. I told God if I saw her, I would lay these hands. She even admitted to it. I was so hurt that this entire time I shared my suspicions of my husband cheating on me, she agreed with me (knowing she was the one he was cheating on me with). Y'all, I wanted to beat the living daylights out of her. I hadn't felt like that since back in my teenage years. I used to blackout and come around to realize someone was pulling me off the person I was beating. Not a good space to be in. God didn't allow me to see her for about two years or so. God knows his daughter well because I would have taken all of the anger and pain that I had been through the years out on her. God knew. Of course, Mr. Dub denied it the entire time. I forgave her through the strength of God as though it had never happened.

Mr. Dub and the pastor couldn't understand how I could forgive her and not him. It really took God to help me. It definitely was a long process. I had to pray that God helped me to forgive because I told God I was laying these hands on her if I saw her. I started thinking of Scriptures that would justify my emotions so I wouldn't feel bad for what I was planning. Y'all know how yall church folks do; stop playing and tell the truth! That's why you're laughing right now LOL. I love her till this day as though nothing happened, but I also know my place in her life too. I eventually forgave Mr. Dub as well. When you love God and want to please Him, you will learn that forgiveness isn't about the other person; it is about cleansing your heart from anything toxic. Psalms 24:4 talks about having clean hands and a pure heart. Having a pure heart means not holding grudges, unforgiveness, envy, or strife in your heart, as this makes your heart toxic. We have to learn how to love from a pure space which isn't very easy in most cases. This is when He has to allow Christ to be born in us.

Anyone that has experienced birth understands that it is very painful; but, once the pain has left, it's like, *what pain?* Forgiveness is the same way—*true* forgiveness. It's like it never happened. You can see that person and love them genuinely. Now, would I ever bring my man around her again? No. Will I ever talk to her about my relationships? No. When things like that happen, you just add boundaries, especially if that person is assigned to you. Some relationships are assigned to you, and you can't just cut them off. God will continue to put them in your spirit to pray for and cover them. You're responsible for them. Even if they don't want to receive you or listen to what God tells you to tell them. They will come back, apologize privately, and repeat the message God told them through you. You have to love them and go on. At the end of the day, you must obey what God tells you. Your next level is based on your level of obedience. And that is what He tells you so he can qualify you for the next level. We have to allow Christ to be born in us.

Chapter 7:

SPIRITUAL DEATH

Now, I found a church that seems to have balance. The pastor came from the church I originally started with, Higher Dimension, so I felt more comfortable and at home. Praying was part of my routine. Every day, when the girls got home, I would help with homework, cook, and prepare them for bed. Whenever the church had prayer, I was there; no matter how early or late, my girls were right there with me.

I stayed out at the church to avoid getting into trouble and having sex with an ex-boyfriend. I was in a space where I just wanted God and was doing everything I could to ensure I stayed right in His eyesight. When they asked for help to lay the church carpet, the young lady who introduced me to the church and I ran to help. We were the only two women present, so we got down and dirty. This was at least six to seven months after my ex-husband and I went our separate ways.

I had been attending this church for a while now, just in the background—receiving and healing. The worship was bomb, and the anointing was strong in every service. You could feel the anointing of God. I felt deliverance in this church and fell in love with the ministry. I had always wanted to praise dance.

This church had a young lady that danced so gracefully under the anointing. I admired her so much. After I had been at the church for a while, I joined the praise dance team. It was a lot of fun. My first time was at the Kingdom Leaders Conference with Bishop Myles Monroe. I really enjoyed dancing for the Lord.

By this time, I had met a young lady named Abby! I love her for life. She was my *ride-da*. She would go ham on my behalf just from her watching me from afar. She would just come and love on me and speak life into me. I remember there was a women's encounter camp, and she asked me to dance. I was like, *really*? And she said yes. So, she spoke to the bishop's wife, who was in charge of the women's encounter, and asked if I could dance; she said yes. I was super nervous.

I didn't know what song to dance to until I was in prayer. I asked God to make me over as I was singing this song by 'Tonxe.' I devised a routine for the song, called Abby, and showed her during the rehearsal. She loved it. Well, after dancing for the women at the encounter, I didn't know that Abby had requested me to dance on Sunday morning too. I peed in my pants. I was soooooo, soooo nervous. The feeling of someone believing in me that much made me emotional, and it still does to date. I was trembling on the inside.

Sunday morning came, and after praise and worship, they announced that I would go up before the bishop. My stomach dropped with worry because my dance wasn't that great to me. Yet, when praise and worship finished, and the announcements were over, I was up next. I said a little prayer to myself and allowed God to have His way. So I got up there and started dancing to the song. Right before the song was over, people started coming to the altar; like, *lots* and *lots* of people. I started crying, praising God cause He used something I wasn't even great at to draw people to the altar. Man was upset. She asked, "Who told her she could dance without asking me?" Boy, she was upset. She had an attitude with me because not only did God use me that time, but I had started traveling with the bishop.

The assistant pastor wasn't fond of my dancing because it looked unprofessional. For some reason, the bishop no longer asked me to travel to dance. I was fine with that, LOL, because I wasn't that comfortable doing it. The good thing is I was able to do something I always wanted to do.

There were so many things I loved about this church; it was peaceful, had a balance, and people spoke prophetically from time to time to the congregation. We would have prophetic guests such as Pastor Bennett at the time. I used to love it when she came to the church. We also had altar calls: people were being delivered and set free at the altar. Praise and worship was everything. I loved the church so much that I started getting involved in what they called "Journey To Purpose." It was a program for new members and everyone who had been to an encounter. Encounters were so powerful. I remember feeling so light, like a feather. I felt most powerful in God during these times. I would wake up EVERY morning at 5:30

am, and pray, worship, and read my Word. I started seeing clearer than I had in a long time. It felt so good. God and I became closer, and my confidence was at its height. I started becoming more acquainted with different ones.

I started working in the bookstore. I was at EVERY prayer meeting at the church, no matter how early or late. Me and my girls. My girls hated it, but it didn't matter. Anytime they needed a volunteer, I ran to the church to occupy myself, so I wouldn't meet a man and get distracted from what God was doing in my life or do something I didn't have any business getting into. So, I found every opportunity to be at the church. This is how I met my late husband, Jr.

He would come up to the church during his lunch break and talk to all of us that were laying the carpet. We would all laugh and have fun with the bishop. He was very fun to be around and easy to talk to. We had a lot of fun learning how to lay the carpet. Most of the time, me and the lady who recommended the church used to lay the carpet. I still remember till this day putting those hard pads on my knees so they wouldn't hurt from being on that hard concrete that was under the old carpet. It was an adventure.

From that point, Jr. and I would speak occasionally, but he would watch me from afar. I didn't even know that he noticed much about me outside of the small talk we would have when I worked in the church bookstore (where we duplicated service to be sold after every service we had). He would come back there, pick up a CD, and chop it up with us in the bookstore. He did this for a while, not realizing he was secretly getting to know me. He was a man of few words. After watching for some time, he finally asked me for my number but not to date me. I can't quite remember because so much happened during our time together, but we had to fight to prove our love for each other. And boy, did we put up a helluva fight; from the middle of 2006 all the way till his dying day.

You see, what I didn't know at first was that he was seven years younger than me. He had an old soul. He was funny but a man of few words. When he spoke, he did so with authority and confidence. After he took my number, I didn't know that he went and spoke to his parents and siblings about me way before he approached me. So, when I finally met his parents, his mother "appeared" warm and nice. Dad was standoffish but said hello and didn't speak much after that. I remember Jr. convinced me to let his mother take me to eat with Kim. I will never forget how she started off in prayer and opened the Bible. I can't remember if she called herself ministering to me with wisdom or what.

The white family didn't know I had a very close relationship with God and was acquainted with Him and His ways. I had good discernment then, and God blessed me with the gift of emotional empathy. So, whenever she had a daughter come to pick my spirit up, I would allow her to do so. Yes, I said *allow* because I knew how to close my spirit, so no one was able to read it. So, when Jr. told me to take a ride with his mother and Kim to talk, I had already discerned their intentions. After his mom was done "speaking," she slammed her hand down on that Bible and said, "Over my dead body. You two will *not* be." I just looked at her, shook my head, held my peace, and went on my way.

For the first time, I really sought God about Jr. and I's relationship (and so did he). We agreed to both fast separately for a week and then tell each other what we heard from God or what He may have shown us in a dream. Once we concluded our fast, we both stated we wouldn't have sex before marriage and had peace knowing God brought us together. We told each other everything so no one could hold anything against us or break our trust in each other by hearing things from other people first. He shared some very personal things with me about his childhood and adult life and the people he may have liked or dated. I shared everything I was ashamed of, especially being married many times.

I remember sharing my heart with him, and he looked at me with tears in my eyes and said it just takes someone to wipe the dirt off me so they can see the treasure that I really am. I will never ever forget this; like, never in life. Not only did he see the treasure, but he also made me go back to school, and he went back with me. He was my support; he pushed me out at church by making me work on the altar, and pulled all the good stuff out of me. We prayed together and shed some tears. He taught me never to let anyone stop me from being who I am by taking me out of my character as a woman of God. We fought to stay together. No one agreed with our decision to be together, but we stood firm.

However, I was stressed. Every time his parents came to town, they wanted everyone to come together. I would beg Jr. not to make me go. It was so uncomfortable. They ALWAYS brought his ex-fiancé around. Like yall, I can't make this up. They would take her shopping and get her hair done as Jr. liked it. They were using her to stop us from the decision we had made as a couple. Like we NEVER, and I mean NEVER, spent time with just us and his family. They never bothered to know me or anything about me. Like how funny I am, how loving I am, how forgiving I am, or how real I am. I don't know how to fake. With me, what you see is what you get. I don't pretend for NO ONE. Very unfortunate for them.

His parents lived in Germany. When people come into town, you want to spend time with them, but they couldn't and wouldn't separate his ex-fiancé's time from ours. She meant it when she said, 'over her dead body.' When I said his family tried it ALLLLL, baby, let me tell you...he would go off on them. The Lord had shown me that his family thought I had him acting like that when I was telling him to cut it out the entire time. I told him he was making it harder for me because his family thought I had him acting like that, and that's why they thought I was the devil.

Honey, his mama was something. She would send out these family emails, include me in them, and talk about how the devil was dividing her family. Boy, I tell you, people become delusional when things don't go their way. So much so they were willing to go dig something up from my past, hoping that revealing this so-called bad thing would turn Jr. away from me.

I will never forget as we were planning our wedding...wait... hold up, let me backup for a minute. I gotta tell it *all*. I know y'all like, *hold up. How did we get to talking about a wedding?* My bad, my bad. LOL, hahaha. So, on my birthday on October 24th, 2006, Jr. asked me to be his girlfriend. He cooked me dinner at his house. He bought me a Bible and a few books by Joyce Myers on the issues I was dealing with personally. On February 14, 2007, he bought me a Swarovski Crystal watch and a Coach purse. In May 2007, he proposed to me. This was followed by drama because he gave me the ring he had bought for his ex-fiancé. I wasn't tripping because it was my favorite diamond, and that was the type of ring I had asked God for. But boy, did his family have their draws in a wad. Because this person that was close to Jr. was a pastor, they talked with my pastor and told him what THEIR truth was. But it wasn't quite the facts.

Now, the church was involved with half of a story, and I was being attacked. By this time, we had become ministers in the church. We worked that altar, and people came back with testimonies of how God blessed them. God was using me to bless their life so they could glorify Him. The words God would give me for them during prayer would come to pass, and different people came back with testimonies.

Some of them in higher positions said I wasn't a prophet and that I could only speak to different ones because of the anointing of the house. I didn't care because I hated titles; all I cared about was that the people of God were blessed. I knew it wasn't about me and what people thought of me. I knew it was about God using me for those who needed and wanted Him. My prayer has always been that I would be a reflection of God, so much so that when people saw me, they would see Jesus and glorify Him. After attending a women's encounter, my spiritual life started blooming. I felt light as a feather and maintained my prayer life every morning at 5:30 am. I saw my gifts develop more, and I could see in a way I'd never seen before.

As time passed, this lady joined the church out of nowhere. She appeared with her real name and then asked us to start calling her "Prophetess." I was like, *what happened to your name?* Out of nowhere, she became a part of the leadership team, using her gift to try and change things.

I remember when she walked over to me before service one day and said, "Why is God angry that I am coming to you? I should have known right then that she was not of God. Then she said to me, "Why aren't you doing what God told you to do?" I'm like, *"What He told me to do!?"* I just looked at her. I still wasn't sure about her. I just knew something about her didn't sit right with me. Because I trusted the leadership of the house, I questioned what I was feeling because I was still growing in my gift. I came to know her more through this young lady who was cool with Jr. She would talk about how the prophetess would help them and speak life into them so much that this young lady and her husband took to her.

The ole girl prophetess came to me one day and started ministering to me through the Word of knowledge; she was accurate, which made me think that I was off until one morning during my prayer time and reading the Word. I had gotten a vision of a black widow in a large spider web, and God had shown me her face. It was as if God was warning me. By this time, Jr. and I had started marriage counseling with her. I remember she started asking weird wonder-if questions like, "Wonder if someone gets left at the altar...wonder if Jr. got really sick...wonder if he needed to go to the hospital...who would watch your children? What would you do if you lost everything?" They started feeling like *real* questions.

After this counseling session, I went to the Lord and talked to Him about this situation. I started thinking she was the devil himself. But I was like, *"God how can she be the devil and prophesy accurately to me?"* The Lord told me, "The devil has to obey me. He just takes the information and attempts to do the opposite with it." I was like, WOW. God started teaching me something else about gifts. I told Jr. that she was a witch and we needed to stop going to her, but he didn't listen to me. She had turned him against me regarding her. I pleaded with him to stop talking to her, but he kept on because she was accurate, appeared to be sweet, and the ole girl had a husband. I believe till this day that one of her sons is Jr.'s. He looks just like him. Yeah, I loved Jr. but yeah...that's later in this story. Going back to the girl that called herself a prophetess...

I used to be close to this woman of God. Let's call her LM. She had also picked up something by the spirit, and we discussed it. We both saw the same thing. One morning, ole girl prophetess called, asking me to come to breakfast. I'm like, "Yeah, I'll come to breakfast, but I'm leaving my girls at home." She agreed. I arrived and sat at her kitchen table as she cooked (knowing I wasn't about to eat anything she was cooking). Y'all hear me...*nathing*?! She was standing at the kitchen sink washing dishes, and started asking these crazy questions; however, this day, I was ready. So she says she wonders if *I'm* the devil. I go, "Well, it is funny that you ask that question because I was wondering if *you* were the devil." Like y'all, I can't make this up. Then she goes on to say, "Wonder if I was here to destroy you both: you and Jr." I then said, "Are you?" She started looking out the window, saying, "Yeaaa, to kill you both. How are you going to pray?"

The devil was asking for responses so he could counteract whatever I said. Then, she mentioned the wedding again, "Wonder if someone gets left at the altar..." She was telling me the enemy's plan for Jr. and I's wedding and our lives collectively. Like y'all, I was like, *"This is not real"* in my head. Because there was so much going on around our wedding and just us being together, I couldn't tell anyone about what had transpired. All I could do was try to convince Jr. to disconnect from this witch; but, she had him so fooled he didn't listen to me. He believed she was a lamb, and I'm like, dude, she is a *wolf.*

As time went by, Jr. got his mom to do marriage counseling with us. I was like, dude she is not *for us.* She had an agenda to compare me and his ex-fiance (she didn't want him to marry her either). She was hoping that he would marry her armor bearer but was using his ex-fiance to attempt to draw him away from me. I saw she was playing both sides and said something openly in front of Jr. and his ex-fiance. Y'all should have seen the look she gave me. I felt like I was in a real-life soap opera. She was stressing me out so bad I started shedding weight. I didn't even realize I was losing weight until our pastor at the time said something about it—but it still didn't register to me. Y'all, I looked like a little Rat Terrier dog in the face. LOL, go ahead and laugh. I know that mess is funny as heck. Like, I was a size four in my wedding dress. Yes, 5'8 1/2 weighing 114 pounds.

Chapter 8:

THE WEDDING

The sad thing about it is Jr. never realized how much all of this drama was stressing me out. Boy, how I am sooooo, sooooo so glad we decided not to have sex until we had gotten married. Jr. was having medical issues, such as blood appearing in his urine. All of this was going on before we got married. My mother and I had urged him to go get checked because that wasn't an issue to play with.

He started experiencing this problem while we were engaged. He was so focused on work that he wouldn't go to the doctor until my mother and I explained the seriousness of seeing blood in his urine. He didn't have any medical insurance yet, so he went to a clinic where I thought he had blood work done. They only gave him medication for the blood in his urine. He went to several appointments at this clinic. He seemed okay for a lil bit.

Jr. was so stubborn (much like me), yet very determined. He graduated from ORU with a double degree; a brilliant young man who was also an accountant at an oil company. He was fine too, y'all. He was tall, dark, handsome, and slightly bow legged—looking like Morris Chestnut. We had a lot of fun with each other until all the other drama entered. Jr. had big plans for our wedding. We wanted to use our wedding for the glory of God by having a small altar call because we understood that we might have some guests that may never step into church again. We both strongly desired to see souls saved for *real*.

Jr. would do these daily journal emails. They were powerful and impactful. The only thing is that he didn't realize God was speaking to *him*. He thought he was writing down things for other people and not himself. I felt his heart hurt during all the drama and fighting we had to do just to be together. I believe he was hurt that certain people would do whatever was necessary to FORCE THEIR will—not caring about what souls they were damaging. Children could be scared by all of this. All they cared about was what would not happen over their dead body and not allowing anyone to ruin the image of how their family might seem (even if it were for their own children). They were willing to go beyond and above even if it meant ruining someone's image and reputation. Like y'all, I can't make this up.

Let me tell you. If you could, remember my first husband and that entire situation, how I was poor, and how the judge granted my divorce in a court docket because I was too poor to afford a divorce decree. Y'all, this mess is funny. This person thought they had something on me but didn't know about this piece of paper I had carried for years. So, during our wedding, everyone was waiting on Jr. and me. These people were walking around the church, saying *this will not happen*. Like y'all, for real. They were loud too: praying in tongues, hahahahaha, thinking all that was going to stop Jr. from marrying me. These crazy people went looking for everything they could find. Wait, let me tell you this real quick…

Y'all, I can't make this up. Jr. had asked a pastor he was friends with to officiate the wedding. The pastor had agreed until this individual called him and told him how many times I had been married (thinking Jr. didn't know). See, I had told him *everything*. He was my best friend. So, this pastor called Jr. while I was sitting on the bed. He asked Jr., "Did you know how many times she has been married?" He said, "Yes, and she told me why," and explained it to him. After that, the pastor decided not to officiate the wedding. He did not show up.

This person was going over and beyond to make sure THEIR WILL would come to pass (which is witchcraft). This was demonic behavior at this point. Their prayers were not working, so they had to take control by doing things in their flesh. They would try to use the Word, and I would just look at them because God had told me it wasn't Him speaking; this person didn't like that about me. This person could not control my mind like they told me they could with Jr.—control how he thinks. This person said this out loud. I was like, *do you hear yourself?* SMH…so, that didn't work.

Jr. asked our pastor to officiate the wedding, and he agreed. Now all this time, I was like, "Mr. Jr., we can wait. We do not have to be in a rush," but he was adamant that the Lord said we should get married on July 7th. I asked, "Are you sure?" He said, "Yes." So, I just followed. Now back to the wedding day, I had to give y'all that lil background to show you how DESPERATE this person was to make sure THEIR will manifested so they could say, "See, I told you this *wasn't* God."

While my dad was taking pictures of the groom, his posse, me, and my girls, someone came and said they just asked Jr. to go to the back office. All I could think about was what the witch said: *someone would be left at the altar.* Then somebody came and grabbed me and said, "They want to see you in the back." All you could hear were these particular people saying, "This is not going to happen." I was like, *okay, God, what's going on?* Now y'all, my Dad has always been laid back, doesn't start trouble, and is really cool. (Pause) I need to say this so I won't forget. My family and friends were in town from LA. Okay, I needed to say that before moving on. All I could see was my daddy walking around saying, "All I know is, y'all messing with the *wrong* daughter. This is *my* daughter." However, it was the *way* he was saying it; it was giving me all kinds of life. I was like, *okay, daddy. Okay, my daddy a G!*

My Daddy was ready to scrap with no fear in his bones. I'm like, this is where I get this from. My mama was also low-key. She may have been short, but she was a fireball with no fear in her bones. So, Jr. and I came in, and they looked at me and said, "You are still married to your first husband." They pulled out this paper that had been printed off seven days before my wedding day. Let me say that one more time: this piece of paper was printed off (y'all hear me), *seven days before our wedding day.* This was malicious.

Y'all ready for this? Naw, y'all ain't ready. You know what else they did? Now, I told you I had proof of my divorce and just needed to go to the house and pick it up. So, while I was getting the paperwork to prove this information was false, the person announced it to all the guests. Y'all ready? Y'all ready for this? They said that Jr. and I would not get married because I was still married to my first husband. *What type of deformation mess was this?* Jr. was hot; he was ready to sue the church.

I heard God say it was a trick of the enemy to give me a bad reputation and blame us for the church's misfortune. I told him what the Lord told me. He still wanted to get married, but I just prayed. After I brought the proof and showed our pastor the legal documentation that I was divorced, he said he wouldn't marry us. So we said, okay. He also said we couldn't use his church, and we said okay. Y'all just don't know. If I had responded to all that in my old self and had not been calm, my family and friends would have torn that church up. My friends and family who had flown to Tulsa to attend our wedding weren't saved. They were *ready*, and it would have been on and cracking. God had given me peace. I learned that day what peace that surpasses all understanding felt like!

I calmly spoke to everyone as they checked on me to see if I was okay. I told them not to cut up—I was good. Like y'all, I can't make this stuff up. Jr. wasn't playing; he *was* marrying me. He wasn't trying to hear me when I said we could wait. He gave me this look and said we are not giving in to the devil's plan. I had a friend that was a licensed minister. I asked her if she would marry Jr. and I, and she said yes. So, we moved everything to our apartment, and got married there with my friends and family. None of his family were a part of the wedding in our apartment. That day ended beautifully.

We went to bed peacefully, not knowing we would have a baby. Oh yeah, I forgot to tell you guys that I was so stressed out that the only thing I hadn't told Jr. was that my tubes were tied. So, I told him three days before the wedding to get him to put it off. He took what I said to the Lord, returned, and told me that the Lord told him I could have children. I don't care what anyone said; Jr. was able to hear from God. So much so that after a few months, he came to me and said the Lord told him I was pregnant. I looked at him and told him I was not pregnant.

Later on, I had him drive me almost two and a half hours for some tacos from Jack in the Box. I craved them a lot while I was pregnant. So much that I called the corporate office and asked them if they could mail me tacos. I sure did. Go ahead and laugh! That mess was funny. He would take me to get tacos quite often. However, at this time, I had not realized I was pregnant. So finally, I agreed to go to the parenthood expecting mothers to get a pregnancy test done.

We walked into the room, and they had me pee into a cup. Jr. and I were waiting in the room for the results. That doctor came in that room and said, "You all know the results." I said,

"I am not pregnant?" Then he said, "No ma'am, you *are* pregnant. You got pregnant on 7/7," (our wedding night). I guess all the waiting had built up to something. Jr. was happy. I told him that we were having a boy. He was like, "You don't know," and I said, "Yes, I do, because I told God I didn't want any more girls and that I would love to have a boy."

Now, y'all ready for this? If you are standing up, have a seat because what I am about to tell you, I can't make this up. Let me back up again…so, one of Jr.'s family members called me and asked me what my friend's minister license number was for the state of Oklahoma. I gave this person the information, and she thanked me. A little later, she called Jr. and told him that our marriage wasn't real…you heard what I said. She told him *our marriage wasn't real.* Now, my friend had been a minister for quite some time, so I was like, *when does a person stop?* Like good Lord, go have 2 seats, please, and thank you. She just refused to accept our marriage.

I didn't fit the image of the wife she pictured for her son (and little did the ex-fiancé know that she wasn't her pick either). She was just playing both sides. I felt like I was living a soap opera in real life. OMG, y'all, she wouldn't stop. She called almost every day, saying our marriage was not real—not only to us, but to the leaders at my church. She was delusional. Like this is a lot; was she mentally unstable? She doesn't know I know this, but Jr. went and saw his ex-fiancee; this still didn't work. At this point, I'm pregnant, and now I'm showing. I was so stressed I almost lost my son. God had shown me that certain people were praying that I would lose the baby.

One day while serving at the church (yeah, I still was serving at the church through all of this), I felt like I was about to start my period. I went to the bathroom and saw blood going down my leg. I hurried up and went home and called this young lady that was like my spiritual big sister. She told me to go home, put my feet up, and plead the blood of Jesus; to speak to my son, and tell him he shall live and not die.

The doctors had taken me off work because my tubes were tied, making me high risk. Man, I went *in*. I started rubbing my belly and talking to my baby at the same time. I used to sing and read the Word to him every day/night. As time went by, he became so active in my stomach. Different people would approach me and ask me what I am having. I would say a boy. Then the next question was, "How do you know? Have you gotten an ultrasound yet?" I would say no. I had to go off on one person because they told me I was having a girl. I must have looked at them and told them I was not having any girl. God knew how I felt about having another girl. So I knew he wasn't going to make me conceive one.

Then my Jr. came to me and said this person told him I was having a girl because the baby was so active. I must have looked at him and told him, "I don't care how much he's moving around, I am not having any girl. *Period!*" This was so annoying to me. So, we get past me being pregnant, and I am finally pregnant enough to get an ultrasound. I was so excited about this day so I could rub in everyone's face that I was having a boy. When my doctor took a pic of his winkie, I said, "Yesssssss."

I looked at Jr. and said, "*I told you* we were having a boy." Man, we went to church. I couldn't wait for someone to come ask me what I was having.

Let me explain something before I go on. So, even though I was pregnant, I still wore my heels to church and still dressed cute because I just wouldn't have it any other way. I had forgotten the time the Holy Spirit hit me, and I started dancing with my big stomach and high heels on. All I could hear the bishop saying was to make sure she was okay. Everyone was trying to make me sit down. But when you think of the goodness of the Lord and know the Lord has you, you'll get to shouting with no fear too. I remember back in my early twenties. I had surgery and didn't want to miss church. I told myself I'm just going to sit down because I had stitches in my stomach. Man, the power of God was so strong at church I started shouting all over that church; and do you know I had not one pain nor a stitch come apart? I'm talking about *God.*

I knew that God would keep our baby boy and me safe while I shouted to give Him all the glory. Because no matter what the enemy tried, his plan would never work. Now, y'all would think by now that this person would say, *okay, let me just accept this marriage at this point*, right? NOPE!!! I can hear some of you saying, "Are you kidding me!?" This person was still going on and on and STILL REFUSES to stop. I forgot to mention that his family stopped coming by the house since our marriage "wasn't real." A sibling would only come by the house if the Oracle had sent them or approved of it. They didn't want to be around me. If someone came by, it was always an agenda—it was never sincere. Now here is the sick part: my daughters from my past relationships/marriage had a social media page. His family would contact them allllll the time, even to this day, but they never asked about their brother's son, who is their nephew. His family accepted my daughters but not me nor my unborn son. Just sick. Isn't this crazy?! Like, denial on steroids. This would make me so angry cause they would say that my daughters were their family but not me???

I know right now, y'all have some popcorn and a drink sitting in your place of comfort, saying to yourself that this is a movie. Or you have made a stopping point saying, *I have to read this when I get home.* Again, y'all already know what I am about to say…"I can't make this stuff up." So, I'm about six months pregnant and very in tune with God, when Jr. comes to me and says that his mom wants us to go to Germany for Christmas. I looked at him and said I'd go, but asked who else was coming? I asked because every encounter we've had with these particular people, his ex-fiancée was ALWAYS involved cause this person just doesn't know how to quit. So, he tells me, "Just the family." I said, "Okay, where are we staying?" Because at this point, I didn't trust any of them as far as I could *see* them. Jr. waited a little and told me where we would be staying; and all of us would go, including my children. So I agreed, hoping we would spend it with immediate family and spouses; no so-called "spiritual daughters" (his ex-fiancée) attending.

So, this person brought us all our passports to head to Germany. I was ready for some possible peace until one day, in my prayer closet, the Lord told me that the ex-fiancée was coming. I said, *all hecks naw, I am not going all the way across the country to deal with what I'm dealing with in the US. AND, I'm pregnant.* I was so annoyed because this person just did not know how or when to stop. Like, this was witchcraft. See, this person thought if they paid for our passports and tickets to go to Germany that nothing would stop me from going overseas because of the amount of money spent in flying to Germany. I'm not one to be played with, nor did I appreciate these physiological games.

So, I looked at Jr. and told him that I, and I mean *I*, would not be going across the water to deal with what I was dealing with in the US (especially while I was pregnant). I told him he could go, but I wasn't coming. That person could just be mad, but it was a no for me. This behavior from this person was soooo bad that Jr. and I couldn't enjoy ourselves because of all the drama and contention she brought because her way wasn't manifesting. I even tried being cool with this person, but she always had a freakin agenda! It was NEVER genuine. This person's control problem was so bad I called her "the oracle," like, people couldn't move unless "the oracle" said so.

See, this person had a prophetic gift and was very accurate at some point in her spiritual walk. So, everyone would listen to her because of her gifts and track record of accuracy. This person was so blinded by THEIR will that they began to say God said things (yet these were coming from her heart). This person didn't realize the god speaking to and through them was the god of PRIDE and self-will. God showed me this person needed a lot of love and was going through things they couldn't trust to discuss with anyone.

This person was hiding behind keeping up a smiling image no matter what; they would not let anyone know what they were going through. At that time, this person was going through a lot on the inside. I remember going to them and trying to minister love to this person, and they just looked at me. The sad thing about all of this is that this person and her family never took the time to get to know me outside of their assumptions.

They depicted me as this devil trying to divide their family, yet they had their god of PRIDE that was operating through them. That is what killed and divided their family. Like, they never hung out with me to see what I was like, what my personality was like, my goofy side, spiritual side—like, nothing. They made an entire decision about me based on an assumption and their fears; the biggest mistake they could have ever made. This was strenuous on my family and my daughters. This person had no clue how their actions damaged my daughter's view of church people and God.

So time went by, and a lot was going on. Now, I was having to deal with Jr. God started giving me dreams about what he was doing around ten every morning. It was so bad that God told me to tell Jr. that if he didn't stop, he would lose his job. He didn't believe me. He even showed me what he was doing in my dreams. I remember when he and I were about to have sex, and I noticed one of his sacks was bigger than the other. God had shown me how it happened. So come to find out, he had a hernia in one of his sacks. Now, mind you, before he and I got married, he had blood in his urine. I thought he had seen a doctor about it, and they ran some blood tests on him.

One Thursday, one of the leaders at our church pulled up to our apartments around 11 am with Jr. in the car. I looked at them like, *why are you bringing him home from work*? Jr. looked at me and said, "My boss came looking for me, but I wasn't at my desk...so, he fired me." SMH. I just looked at him. He was making good money working for an oil company in Oklahoma. And mind you, I couldn't work according to the doctor's orders. He was the only one bringing in money to care for my two daughters, him and myself and now that was gone.

I knew why he had gotten fired. God had me warn him, but he didn't listen. It happened just as I saw it would. Now, Jr. was sending out all these devotionals, but he was not once sorrowful. I could tell that he had stopped talking to this person (it's a gift that I didn't realize God had blessed me with). When people were around others, I could tell by their conversation if they had been around another woman, especially if I learned them well. Like, all of my spiritual senses were so high. I couldn't see how Jr. couldn't tell that the devotions he was sending out to everyone were actually meant for him; he never once thought that God was talking to *him*. One day, I told him that I wasn't reading any of his devotionals anymore because he didn't see himself in any of them. He got mad at me. I was trying to tell him that God speaks to us first, *then* people in most cases. He was in defensive mode.

Chapter 9

HERE COMES THE THIEF

Jr. would tell me how this person constantly let them know he wasn't hearing from God. This made him stubborn, and he fought them because he knew it was God who spoke to him. S,o if anyone reflected this person, his first response was to rebel. He started being mean to his family, and I had to remind him that God is love. By this time, I was eight months pregnant.

Now y'all ready for this??? Y'all are not ready for this. So one day, I came home, I forgot where I went, but I was gone for quite some time. I would wake up every morning and play my worship CDs on the cd player. Now, we would listen to music during "clapping time", but I had removed all those CDs from the CD player and replaced them with worship CDs. Now, I came home and saw that the door was cracked open. I looked at him like, *has someone broken into the house?* (Ooh, I forgot to tell y'all, I am a NEAT FREAK, so I know where everything is). I'm looking at him like, *why is he not tripping?*

So, he stands in the kitchen while I look through the house. I'm looking, and our bathroom light is on. The CDs in the CD player were secular music. So I look at him, and he tells me,

"Your watch is still in there, isn't it?" I looked at him like, *I know this fool ain't have nobody in my house AND bed.* Now, my spirit was stirring up and God told me he was lying to me. He was here earlier. I looked at him and asked, "Who were you here with earlier?" He started throwing me off saying, "I'm not the other guy that did you wrong," and all this other stuff. I'm still pregnant, so I gave him this look in his eye, showing him I knew he was lying, and walked away. I didn't even eat that night; Jr. made him and the girls something to eat. I just released it into God's hands.

Jr. started coming home with a stroller and things for the baby, and I was like, *who bought this?* It just wasn't sitting right in my spirit. At this point, I had to just take it to God in prayer. Jr. had been job hunting and wasn't lucky until I suggested he try a temp agency. He contacted this one temp agency, and they hired him. It was paying as well as the oil company. He started having a runny nose and a cough, but we just thought it was the flu and that it would pass. I woke up every morning to cook breakfast for the house, made him tea to take to work, and called him at work to make sure he didn't need me to bring him anything.

I just wanted us to find some peace. We never had the time to enjoy our marriage because of the outside noise and distractions. You would think people would just back up and allow God to be God. See, God wasn't working in their favor, so they had to *become god* by doing everything they could to make their will come to pass. Did you know this person had the nerve to tell me that their armor bearer/daughter (not ex-fiancee) wanted a boy, and when she found out that I was having a boy, she was heartbroken? Because *she* wanted to have a boy for Jr. (she already had a few children by her lay husband). OMG, I was like, *are you kidding me right now*? I just wanted to love Jr. and my children while doing the work of the Lord.

Things started looking brighter at this point. We prayed together in the mornings. I cooked breakfast for everyone, made sure the girls ate before school, helped them with homework, and cooked dinner before 6 pm. I was big on making sure the girls had structure and were giving their all in school. Both my girls were on the honor roll and were very intelligent with their smart "A" mouths LOL.

Eventually, Jr. found another job as an accountant. I was excited for him. Then a month into his new job, he started behaving the way he did when he worked for the oil company. I just prayed at this point because I had to be happy for my girls and my little guy, who was due in March (which was just a couple of months away). I was so hurt cause I could see so clearly, but I didn't believe anyone should leave someone because of infidelity. I understood that the enemy was on a mission, and I wouldn't let him win, so I prayed during my quiet time and told God all about it. I've seen Him work so many times that I wasn't worried about him fixing it. I was just concerned as to how long it would take.

We were faithful members and ministers at our church. I was pregnant but was still faithful to the call on our lives. Jr.

would make me sit in that front row every Sunday. He wasn't having it any other way, y'all hear me? I understood how sacred the altar is, so when I felt my spirit wasn't right, I did not want to sit in front of the church. I knew how to shift. I would start worshiping and block out everyone around me and spend time with my Daddy God as I would do at home. I knew how to tune everyone out by looking at the ceiling and telling God how much I loved and adored Him. If He never did another thing in my life, He was still an amazing and faithful God that I would forever serve.

During this time, one of Jr.'s siblings started selling life insurance and told everyone he knew about it. Jr. didn't want to do it at first cause he wasn't sure if it was legit. So, I told him it wouldn't hurt to help them since they were just starting a new business. We could support them as family, even though they wouldn't come over any other time. I did my best to reflect God's love despite how others may have treated me.

Jr. was still having flu-like symptoms. They weren't going away, so I suggested he go to the doctor. He hated taking time off work, but I convinced him to go. He made an appointment to see what was going on with him. We went and found out that he had walking pneumonia. They gave him some antibiotics to clear it up. He still went to work and church. I made sure he had lemon and honey tea every morning, and a healthy breakfast to help build up his immune system. Noe, we were dealing with his hernia and walking pneumonia. Yeah, hernia! One evening, when we were about to have sex, I realized one of his sacks was huge. It was the size of a golf ball. I looked at him and said, "How'd you do that?" He couldn't really answer me, and it turned me off. I asked again, and he said, "It's just a hernia." I was shocked and thought, *Just a hernia!? Who saw this to tell you that it's just a hernia?* That is what I said in my head. At this point, I was like, *Oh Lord, please help me.*

Jr. was frustrated, so he got checked to see what could be done about his hernia. I told him, "Babe, let's allow this pneumonia to clear up before doing something about your hernia," but of course, he could be as stubborn as a mule when he wanted to be. He went ahead to see a doctor about the hernia and was told he needed surgery. I begged, and begged him to please wait until the flu passed. "Please wait, baby, *please,*" I said, but he scheduled an appointment for the surgery anyway. Of course, I really went into prayer because I felt in my spirit he should have waited until he was completely healed. The pneumonia was going away, but it had not cleared up all the way. In spite of his decision, I was still a supportive wife. So, he went to his appointment for surgery.

I remember the nurse had his blood checked right before surgery. When the results came back, the nurse said Jr.'s blood was low and that we should wait for her to speak to the surgeon about it. The nurse stated that we might have to reschedule his surgery due to his low blood count. The surgeon, on the other hand, said he would still perform the surgery. I had no peace in my spirit about this, but I just had to pray for God to cover him. Jr. was not hearing anything the nurse was saying about rescheduling. He wanted *what* he wanted, *when* he wanted it, and no one was stopping him from getting it.

He underwent surgery, and I brought him home to take care of him. I used to take care of and nurture people for a living. My medical background helped me discern what wasn't medically normal. As two days passed, Jr. was laying on the couch where he stayed because he had to be propped and lie a certain way. I realized his legs had started swelling abnormally. I looked at him and said, "Honey, I'm concerned your legs are swelling. This doesn't look normal." He told me the doctor said he would have some swelling, which was normal. I looked at him and told him my spirit was disturbed. If the swelling didn't go down within the next couple of days, I would take him to my DOCTOR, *PERIOD*!!!

A couple of days had gone by and the swelling hadn't gone down. My spirit was really disturbed. He had been going to a medical clinic that took patients, and payments were on a sliding scale. I called my doctor and asked how much cash it would cost to see a new patient. He gave me the price, and I asked him to make an appointment as soon as possible. Well, my doctor had a partner he shared the office with and referred me to them because he was out of the office and couldn't see Jr. that soon. So, I agreed to the appointment.

The Holy Spirit told me to ask Jr. if the doctor had ever drawn his blood. He looked at me, and you know what he said y'all? NO! I was hotter than a firecracker and started fussing and going off. I was pissed. Like, with all these issues going on with Jr., from seeing blood in his urine to now walking pneumonia; a blood test was the first thing a nurse or doctor should have considered. So I told him, "When we go to my doctor, we will get your blood checked." Ooh, y'all, I was hotttt and pissed all at the same time. So, we went to see my doctor's partner, and he told me he didn't see anything wrong with Jr. He prescribed him some water pills. I must have looked that doctor in the eyes and told him, "We are not leaving this office until you order him a blood test TODAY!" He kept saying, "I don't think that is necessary." I looked at him again with a tone in my voice and said, *"I don't care what you think is necessary; we are not leaving this office until you give him a blood test TODAY."*

He saw my seriousness and said, "Okay, I'll go ahead and make an order, but I don't think it's needed." He ordered blood lab work to be drawn and gave me his water pills. I took them but knew I wouldn't give them to him because something else was wrong with him—he was being misdiagnosed. We went home, and early that morning, *I will never forget*: Jr. was laying in bed when the phone rang. I picked it up, and the voice on the other end said, "Hello, is this Mrs. White?" I said, "Yes, it is." He told me, "This is Doctor D." I said I knew who he was. He then asked me if I was giving Jr. those water pills, and I said no, I was not. He then says, "Good. I need you to rush your husband to Hillcrest Hospital because his kidneys are trying to shut down."

He told me not to drive the car. Instead, I should call an ambulance to come pick him up. I had a newborn baby and two young girls while this tragic thing was happening. I went into the room, looked at Jr., and in my calm voice, said, "Honey, that was the doctor. Your blood work came back in. Your kidneys are trying to shut down on you, so we need to go to Hillcrest Hospital in an ambulance." Jr. sat up on the side of the bed and said in a very angry voice, "The devil is trying to kill me. Ooooh if I die, ooooh if I die…" I looked at him and told him to stop professing death. We had a son and girls to raise. He was only twenty-eight years old. At the time, our son was only three months old. I called the ambulance and helped him to get dressed so we could go to the hospital. I called his family members living in Tulsa to tell them we were on our way to the Hillcrest Hospital. I informed them what the doctor said about Jr.'s kidneys trying to shut down.

The hospital was waiting for our arrival, and they took him straight back to the ER. Many doctors and nurses started coming into the room asking Jr. lots of questions: such as how old he was, and if he had any illnesses in the past. They were trying to figure out the cause of his kidneys trying to shut down. I started telling the doctor that he was urinating blood before we got married, and while married, he ended up having walking pneumonia. Then, he had a hernia in one of his sacks, which was why he had gotten surgery done a few weeks ago.

See, Jr. was born in Texas but raised in Germany because his parents were in the military. They were stationed in Germany longer than anyone who served in the army. God had graced them to be raised in an amazing country. While growing up in Germany, Jr. had a rash that appeared on different spots on his body. I believe it was in his blood because when we became intimate, those spots would appear on me for like a day or two and then go away after a few days. They said it was a fungus, but it eventually went away. I never saw this again.

So, the doctors started asking me how old Jr. was and if he had any problems because they couldn't believe someone so young was having these health issues; this was about his kidneys attempting to shut down. First, they drew his blood to see if anything would show up in his red and white blood cells. Sure enough, his white blood count was very high, which meant his body was trying to fight off something. The doctors started running all types of tests to see what may be causing his kidneys to shut down. Different specialists started coming and explaining the types of tests they were running to rule out what could be wrong because they believed he was too young to have kidney issues. All this was going on while he was in the emergency room. They finally told us that they would admit him into the hospital until they figured out what was going on with him. Well, they admitted him to the ICU unit. God had given us favor with the ICU doctor who allowed me to stay in the room with him all day and night.

In the meantime, my girls were at home, and my baby boy was too. My mom stepped in as much as she could to help out with Daniel, and one of my sister's friends helped with the girls. This was very, very hard for me. Like, I had *just* my baby. It tore me up to be away from my babies and even more to be away from my newborn son. I was nursing him as well. My girls couldn't understand why I wasn't at home with them. They thought I chose taking care of Jr. over them. My girls felt like the hospital had nurses and doctors that could look over him. This made it even harder for me.

See, I had worked in health care for some time, and I knew how they were with patients when no one was around. I refused to let anything happen to Jr. (even if things were rough between us due to outside influences). I refused to go home because I wanted to ensure Jr. was getting the right care. Eventually, my godsister came to my house, and a party had agreed to pay her to take care of the children while I was at the hospital with Jr. I would take "bird baths" in his room, and my mom would bring the baby so I could nurse him. We were able to sneak the baby in so Jr. could see him. Thus, we were able to spend time with the little guy. They allowed us to break so many rules because we were a young couple.

A lot happened in our relationship, so we hadn't even enjoyed our marriage that much. It went from me being rejected, to a party fighting us to say our marriage wasn't real, to fighting that my son wasn't his, to Jr. getting laid off from his job for being where he shouldn't have been; I just wanted to scream. It had been one fight after another, but that's not all...

Y'all are not ready for this. When his parents came down, and all hell started breaking loose. Some people just don't know when to freakin quit. Y'all, like, I can't make this stuff up. Before they arrived, I took notes every time the doctor came into the room. I took note of whatever procedure they were going to do, whatever medicine they were prescribing, how often they drew blood for the lab and the lab results. I even had the nurse show me how to read his lab work on the computer. I had refused to leave his side. I told everyone that would come and visit him not to come with no, "woe is me," but to come in good spirits with the hope he was going to get past this.

When his parents arrived, his mother came in and directly attacked me. Like, I was *so* sick of this. I wanted to punch her in her face so many times. Instead, I went to God with tears running down my face, and asked Him to please help me. I also asked God not to let my heart harden and become bitter towards her; to help me reflect the love of Christ no matter how she or anyone else treated me. This was a hard thing to ask, but I wanted God to be pleased with me despite what I was going through. She made me feel like I wasn't worth being loved. She was so mean and sneaky and would hide behind God while doing it. It made me sick to my stomach.

I'm so glad I have a personal relationship with God because if I hadn't, I would have become an atheist because of her. I told her this too. Now it begins…so, she tells Jr. it's my fault he is sick, and Jr. stops talking to me. Because of who I am, it didn't stop me from ensuring he had the highest level of care. Nor did it stop me from serving God. This was their first trip from Germany to see how my Jr. was doing and witness the severity of his illness. While we (myself and his mother) were sitting at the table with the doctor—and y'all are not ready for this—she looked at the doctor right in front of me and said, "Did you give him an AIDS test?" She looked at me as she said it. The doctor said, "Yes, we already gave him an AIDS test, and it came back negative." She then asked if there were different strains of the AIDS test. He said yes, and she then proceeded to ask for him to take another test.

In my spirit, I picked up that she was accusing me of giving my Jr. *AIDS?? WTH! In my face?!* I looked at her and said, "Did you know that Daniel and I were tested for AIDS when I was pregnant? If I were to have had the virus, it would have come up then!" The doctor stated there was no need for another test, but she refused to let it go. The doctor got a little annoyed and had to be firm with his answer by telling her AIDS wasn't the cause of Jr.'s illness.

When this person used to come to me and tell me that the Lord told her stuff, I would hear the Holy Spirit tell me, "It's not me; it's her speaking using my name." I would tell this person what I heard the Spirit saying and that she should stop saying God was telling her these things because she was using God's name in vain. Y'all, it had gotten so bad that my pastor would have to come up to the hospital whenever she was in town. The amazing man she was married to wouldn't say much; he just looked and watched. He was never mean to me, even though he may have had some reservations.

Things had started getting rough with Jr. because they couldn't figure out what was going on with him. The doctor said that he had swollen lymph nodes in several areas of his body and they needed to do a biopsy. While we were in the ICU, they did a biopsy on his bone marrow. Man, that was painful to watch. Remember, the doctor allowed me to stay in the ICU with Jr., and I wanted to see everything they were doing to him. The doctor let me be involved as much as was medically allowed. It was a minor but painful biopsy. Thankfully, Jr. got through it. We waited for the results for almost a day, and they had no luck. The cancer doctor was nice and kept me informed as I had so many questions. I continued to take notes. I observed Jr. throughout this entire procedure. The results came back, and the doctors (he had about four different doctors: the house Doctor, Heart Doctor, Cancer doctor, and a Neurologist) were all nice to us. They couldn't understand how a twenty-eight--year-old young man was going through this.

In the meantime, the girls were upset with me. My mother was still bringing the lil guy so I could nurse him. I prayed over him all of the time. My Princess helped a lot with Daniel, as well as my Angel. My godsister was a lot of help too. She stayed at the house while I was living at the hospital with Jr. to ensure he received the proper care. This was so rough on me. I know only God brought me through all of this. I wouldn't even allow the church to know what was going on with Jr. I would just tell them to keep us in prayer. I didn't need anyone that possessed doubt to add to the fight we were having in regard to Jr.'s health. I prayed and fasted, but it was getting hard.

A few months had gone by, and they still hadn't figured out what was wrong with Jr. He had another biopsy, but this time it was on the lymph, not under his armpit. We waited for those results, but still—nothing. So, I went down to the chapel and asked God what was happening. He said, "I am answering your prayers for everything to come back negative." I went to those who were a part of the family and told them that God said He was answering our prayers because we had been praying for everything to come back negative. Instead, we needed to pray that whatever was going on with Jr. should be *exposed*, so we know how to pray for his healing. This person said to me, "Well, God knows what we mean." I said noooo, cause He wouldn't be telling me how we need to pray.

Y'all, she would get on my dang nerves with her mess. She just always had to be right; trying to continue to prove I couldn't hear from God and only she could. I kept calling her the Oracle because the family wouldn't move unless she okayed it. However, I wasn't having it, and that's why we bumped heads. I knew God for MYSELF. She couldn't manipulate me with Scriptures like she did with Jr. and others.

One morning, I will never forget receiving a phone call from a well-known bishop that was killing it in Texas. His name was Bishop H (rest his soul). He said, "Is this Jr.'s wife?" I said, yes, sir. Then, he started prophesying over me saying, "I don't know you, but I hear the Holy Spirit telling me to let you know that you are a good wife." He said this a few more times, so much that I started to cry. Tears still fall down my face when I remember this; it's even happening now while typing this. Finally, God was showing someone what I was going through.

He would tell me that no weapon formed against me shall prosper, and that my husband would live and not die. He started praying for me and said if I needed anything, I should let him know and also to tell him if anyone was doing me wrong.

He went on to say, "I stand for what is right and God showed me you have a good heart. You are loved by God and woe to anyone that comes against you. I don't care who they are." Now, this bishop was Jr.'s family bishop (as their ministry was under him). Besides my church's assistant pastor, I felt like I was in this walk with Jr. by myself. You would think that because I had a newborn and two children, a family member would offer to relieve me from time to time; but no, they didn't. I would have told them no anyway, but it would have been a nice gesture.

Eventually, a part of Jr.'s family went back to Germany (*thank God*). It was like he would become worse when they were in town, but when they left, he would always start getting better. Even though I was Jr.s wife, a nurse had spoken to Jr. and me. She said that I might want to get a medical power of attorney over Jr. in the event something were to happen to him where he couldn't speak or make decisions for himself. We asked her how we would go about doing this, and she gave us instructions. At this time, Jr. was alert, and I felt peace about leaving him at the hospital while I went to the Office Depot; I picked up a document from there. When I returned, Jr. and I reviewed the document to make sure he was okay with the verbiage. Then we told the lady we were ready to sign and notarize medical oower to me if he couldn't speak for himself.

One part of Jr.'s family returned from Germany because Jr. was scheduled for another biopsy—this time was more of a major surgery. He had to have a biopsy on the lymph, not in his stomach. Y'all are not ready for this…I can't make this stuff up. So, my mother, both pastors from the church (who were associates of Jr.'s other family that were pastors in Germany), plus his family from Germany were all at the hospital. I got called into a room again—just like on my wedding day. It was full of people: Jr.s family, a church member, my two pastors from my church, and the doctor. The doctor started talking, letting us know some of the possibilities in reference to Jr.'s health. Oooooowwwee, y'all not ready; y'all are not ready for *this*. If you're standing up, sit down. The doctor started looking over Jr.'s files to see if we had an insurance policy and a medical power of attorney to make decisions for Jr. if he could not make decisions for himself. While looking through his paperwork, he asked who had power of attorney over Jr. Do y'all know that this person (family member) stood up and said, "He has given me the medical power of attorney in the event something happens to him."

I sat there, annoyed as hell, allowing her to finish saying whatever she was saying. Then I said in a stern but soft voice, "Doctor, if you look further in his paperwork, you'll see that first, I am his wife, and second, I have a notarized paper stating that I am Jr.'s medical power of attorney. I will be making the medical and financial decisions over him." Do y'all know that this woman (family member) stood up and said, *"Over my dead body*! I will go get an attorney to fight this!" I don't remember my response word for word, but I know I said something smart and factual that made his brother say to me not to talk to his family member like that. I told him I would say whatever I wanted to say to her and I was sick of her trying to control stuff. The doctor looked through the paperwork and saw what I was saying. *Can y'all believe this woman?* Like when was this going to stop?

The pastor looked at me, walked me outside the door, and said I handled that better than he thought I would. I told him I was sick of her. Here once more, I was tested again cause my mama and others were at the hospital that day. Had I not handled it, it wouldn't have ended well. Chile, don't make my mama mad; she will go *ham* on you. I know it was God helping me this day. You would think by now that this family member would lighten up. She just got worse and attempted to be sneaky.

Chapter 10

DEATH AND DECEPTION

Now Jr. was no longer in the ICU but in a room. I had someone bring the playpen so we could spend time with our son. He couldn't hold him because we still didn't know what was wrong with him, and his white cell count was getting higher. The doctor would always tell me the orders and prescriptions he was receiving. I would write notes and watch how Jr. responded to the medication. The nurse would come into the room, and I would ask, "What are you about to do?"

I remember a nurse was about to give him platelets. I told her, "That's not in the doctor's orders. Go look at the doctor's orders again." God allowed me to catch a possible mistake and have his medication changed due to his reactions to them. I did not play when it came to taking care of Jr. As a matter of fact, I was his nurse aide. The only thing the nurses had to do was draw blood and give him medications. I did everything else.

Bishop H and his wife had come down to see Jr. Jr. really looked up to Bishop H. He inspired and encouraged me over the phone so it was great seeing him in person. I remember Bishop H, his wife, and some of Jr.'s family members were in the room talking. The bishop randomly said, "Danyle, you are a good wife." He kept saying this repeatedly because this family member refused to hear any good about me. Still, every time she attempted to revert the conversation, he would say it again, "Danyle, you are a great wife, and keep doing what you are doing. You are doing a great job being a wife." She would attempt to change the subject again. This went on for a few minutes.

Then the bishop started speaking to Jr. He broke out this white handkerchief, and started praying over him, saying he shall live and not die. He told him to always wear the white handkerchief. He then looked at me and said, "Make sure he has this on him at all times." I said yes sir. I really appreciated Bishop H. When he left, he called me from time to time, praying and checking up on me. He and a pastor from my church always checked on me and prayed with me. They were so encouraging. Like, they helped me keep my sanity through everything I was dealing with. Every time Jr.'s family members returned to Germany, I had a mental vacation from spiritual and natural attacks—from one family member. She was a thorn in my flesh.

So many times, I called on God to stop the person I was delivered from coming out, whooping her tail, or punching her in the face. I would have fought the entire family and called friends from LA to help me too. I felt like she was the devil in the flesh. She was definitely like a WOLF in sheep's clothing, yet a minister of the Gospel. I was like, *do you read or even know the God you preach about? Do you know the heart of God and how He feels about his children?* She was so spiritually blinded by her OWN will and what SHE wanted for her family that she couldn't even see the enemy using her through her pride and the thickness of her will. And she thought Jr. was getting it from me!? Nah—it was evident who he was like. But, she couldn't see that because she was blinded by what SHE wanted and how SHE wanted it. She did not care who she hurt in the process or who she may be turning away from God.

This was one of the biggest spiritual blows I've ever faced. It was one spiritual blow after another. *But God...*let me say that again, *but God...*I remember going home because I had not been home in months and had to get something from the house. I was driving Jr.'s BMW 5 series, and I had to go up a steep hill to get to our apartment. Well, it was raining that day, and the hill was a lil slippery. I remember sliding down; I braked, and the car almost flipped over. Like y'all, that was one of the scariest things ever, and how the car stopped—no one could have done that but God. I just started praising God and saying, "Thank you, God! Thank you." I ended up going into a prayer of praise. As I look back, I was releasing the pain I was feeling. My heart was so heavy because Jr. was going through so much. He was so young, and we had just had a son that he couldn't even hold. This was so hard on him and me.

Certain family members of Jr.'s couldn't see someone else's pain because they were focused on their OWN WILL. You can't come and say God said all of these things, when God isn't showing you yourself??? Like, you can't tell me you have the Spirit of God and no conviction comes upon you for you to see the damage you are doing to someone else. But y'all know what? In spite of this, I was still nice to this woman because I realized that everyone has a test, and maybe this was mine. I wanted to please God so much that I was willing to let her think whatever she wanted about me. I just wanted to make sure that my heart was right with God. He had been so good to me; I didn't want to disappoint Him. Every time she did something to turn me away from God, I would just tell myself God wasn't doing that to me—she was. Also, church is filled with imperfect people trying to serve a perfect God.

I formed a relationship with the nurses and doctors at the hospital. My mom was bringing the baby to me to nurse. It was hard for me not to be able to see my baby. We had gotten an okay for him to stay in the room during the day. The hospital had put us in a large room so we could have Daniel's playpen and enough room for family and friends to visit. We did this for about a month and a half before the doctors came. They told us that Jr. was going through one more biopsy, but this time it was a major surgery. They had decided to cut him open as a last resort before sending him to the Mayo Clinic back east. At this point, the doctors started making plans to meta-flight Jr. They gave us the details of what would all take place, and what that would look like if they could not find out what was causing his illness. This meant I wouldn't be able to see my son or my girls because I was going with him to ensure he was properly cared for. So, they performed surgery to get a biopsy of a lymph node in his abdominal area. It took a few days. I remember when the doctors came down and said, "We are getting prepared to meet him at the Mayo Clinic in the afternoon." I must have said, "No, he is not; he will get an answer *today*."

I didn't say that out loud, but I walked down to the hospital sanctuary and got on my knees. I prayed to God in faith with authority that the results would come today before they attempted to put him on that helicopter. Sure enough, as I was walking back up, the doctors were walking in to tell us that they finally knew what type of cancer Jr. had. The name of the cancer was called Non-Hodgkin's lymphoma. This cancer was curable. *Yes! Thank you, Jesus.* I started thanking God because now we could pray for his complete healing. They immediately put him on chemotherapy. Now, we were on our way to recovery. My heart leaped for joy. Even though I knew we had a long way to go, I had hope.

Different folks from the church would come to visit and pray with Jr. His barber came by the hospital to shave his head because his hair was falling out from the chemo treatments. I wouldn't allow anyone to visit with an "Oh wow, is this *you*?" attitude toward Jr. This was a form of doubt, and I wasn't having it. I didn't care who you were. As a matter of fact, I fired a few nurses because of it. Y'all didn't know you could fire a nurse from helping you in the hospital? I fired *two*, to be exact. They could help other patients, but not Jr. I didn't play that. I was very protective of him and what was around him. I felt like we were on our journey to recovery. We started having some challenges, but I still believed, no matter what things looked like. I had some resurrecting faith, so no matter what things looked like by sight, I believed that God could do the impossible.

Do y'all know that his family members brought this young lady who was supposed to be a sister back with them from another country? They wanted her to stay at the hospital with Jr. I was like, *dang, when does someone say enough is enough? Jesus!* This family member knew I knew this young lady was in love with Jr. This was not the ex-fiancee; this one was their little secret, but Jr. had already told me about her. This family member snuck her to see him thinking I didn't know about her. She even asked me to run to the house. When I went to the house, she would have his ex come and see him. Let me tell you about God: He will not withhold any good thing from you. He will expose the enemy's hand without the enemy knowing you know.

As tough as it was for God to show me that, I understand they doubted whether he would live or not. You heard me say *they*—his family. In this, I realized that people can preach about God, but when tested to see if they believe what they preach, it shows they only have the knowledge with no true revelation of who God really is. Before he was even close to death, this family member was already planning for it. Some people want their own will so bad they don't care who has to die; that overrides what they desire. This goes back to when I met this family member who stated, "OVER MY DEAD BODY." Like, this person really meant that. This family member refused to accept our marriage. God showed me that when people who ALWAYS want CONTROL lose it, they become OUT OF CONTROL. They would do anything to ensure something didn't exist, even if they had to sacrifice their own. God also showed me that this family member also dabbled in witchcraft, but they tried to use it for good.

Let me tell you something: don't get so caught up in your gift from God that you can't see when your character no longer reflects the truth. Don't ever side with someone just because they claim to be an accurate prophet. If you do, you will never see the error of their ways, and will go along with them like what they say is the Gospel. This is how people are led astray. Now back to what I was talking about...

After his last surgery, the doctors allowed Jr. to come home. We had to get a hospital bed for our room because the regular bed was too flat. I was excited to have him home, but it was very rough on me. I still had to take care of the girls and a new baby that was only about five months old at the time. It was very tough, and I hardly got any sleep. Jr. was very demanding; it was like I was taking care of four children. I had to cook, clean, change diapers, get the girls ready for school, take care of Jr.'s womb, and take him to the bathroom when he needed to go. I had to sleep on the couch so I could hear him calling my name if he needed anything. He got mad at me because I wouldn't rub his feet. He called a family member, who had the nerve to call me, trying to fuss at me.

I was soooo exhausted, and none of his family that lived in town offered to come and help me for a bit so I could get a little rest. One night, I was so extremely tired that I fell asleep on the couch and couldn't hear Jr. calling me. He got out of that bed (that he acted like he couldn't get out of), entered the living room, and woke me up. Listen, he scared the living hell out of me. I was terrified. Do you know he was fussing at me, asking why I was ignoring him? He was just being mean. I had to tell him, "Look, this is rough on me; taking care of you, the girls, and Daniel." Do y'all know that he didn't care about any of that? I was like, *wow*. He was really fussing at me. But I looked at him and said, "I thought you couldn't get out of bed by yourself?" He told me, "I came here to look for you." I replied, "You never considered that I needed some rest and I have a lot of responsibility?" He was like, "No. You're *supposed* to take care of me."

We ended up getting into an argument. Y'all know when you're sleepy-sleepy? As my Madea would say, "Tired folks need to hush…" I was just tired of all the trials I was going through. His family members living in another country were trying to run me and tell me what I needed to do when they had no idea what I was going through. Shoot, I love God, but I have to admit I almost cussed them out. Yet, I would feel God in my spirit while I had tears going down my face. I was like, *Lord, is this ever going to stop?* Like when they were in town, they couldn't even stay at the hospital. *I* had to take him back to the hospital to have dialysis; *I* had to watch what I gave him to eat, plus take care of Daniel and my baby girls.

My mother helped as much as she could, but she had to work. My godsister would come to the apartment and help me when she could. She would cook, play games with the girls, and help me change Daniels's diapers. When she was away, I would call her and talk to her about what was happening. I remember when she came to the apartment, after seeing all that I was going through. She said, "Sis, I have to be honest, I didn't really believe you were going through all that with his family., I have to apologize—like you *can't* make this up. No one should have to go through anything like this." She couldn't believe how strong I was. I was like, "God has been my strength."

I cried to God ALLOTTTTTT. I couldn't believe after all that had happened, that any human being wouldn't see the damage they were doing to someone based on their will not being done. They were willing to do whatever; not caring how it affected someone else. Yet, she was a pastor who said she heard from God. I'm like, God is not telling you or tugging at you to show you what evil you are doing, and how you are possibly scaring a soul just so you can have your way? They were sending their child to my house acting like they were coming to see. Their brother did not know that God would show me this particular sibling's gift and why she was really coming over trying to use some fake wisdom. She had the ability to stand next to someone and read /feel their spirit. She wouldn't come over to our place any other time unless sent by a family member living out of the country. This would happen if the family member thought I was doing something wrong because Jr. was throwing a fit.

Heck, I'm one person taking care of four people and not taking care of myself. This is why I had to go to church to help me keep my mind right so I wouldn't go off on Jr. or any of his family members. I cried so much that I felt I had been acquainted with tears. Outside of going through seventeen years of being destitute, this was one of the toughest seasons of my life. As I look back, I know it was God that kept me.

Now my godsister, the girls, and I were playing cards at the table in the dining area where we could see and hear Jr. if he called or needed anything. This particular night, my godsister said, "Y'all see that?" She was very gifted like my godmother Madea; she could see spirits in their rare form. So I said, "What did you see?" She said, "I just saw a tall demon duck down and walk in the room with Jr. while he was asleep." The night before he had gone to sleep, he was so mean to me. So, I went into his room to see if he was still sleeping, and he was. I just started praying over him, binding and rebuking the devil. When he woke up, I told him a demon had come into his room while he was asleep, and we prayed. His heart had become so bitter and mad at God.

We thought he would be good when he came home for two weeks. Jr. was healing from his last open biopsy, where he had been cut straight down the middle of his stomach and received stitches. I had brought as much from the hospital as I could as far as bandages, wipes, cleaning solution, and ointment for his womb. Since I had worked in the medical field as a Certified Nursing Assistant (CNA), I took excellent care of him as a patient and husband.

I also took down some of the nurses' phone and station numbers in case I needed to call to ask questions (or during an emergency). So, I would do womb care by changing his bandages after I helped him shower each day. One particular evening, I realized this nice size puss bump was bubbling up from his womb from his surgery. I called the doctor, and he told me to watch it and make sure not to bust it because it may be an infection from his surgery.

The next morning as I was helping Jr. sit up from lying down, a burst of water started coming out of his stomach through the puss bump I had noticed earlier. It was like a sidewalk water hydrant at first. It scared the living daylights out of me, and I had to say to myself, *"Get it together."* The Spirit of God shifted my mind and calmed my spirit; I went from panicking and being afraid to *nurse-mode*. It was spurting a large amount of water which wasn't stopping, and the water had a smell. We both were soaked and wet. The floor was drenched with water from his stomach. I remember calling the nurse immediately and asking what I should do to stop the water from coming out of his stomach. It was so much; I didn't know a human being had that much water. The nurse told me to call 911 to get an ambulance to take him back to the hospital. We had been home less than a week after staying in the hospital for two and a half months. So I called 911. This process was hurting my heart and hardening Jr.'s. He started getting so angry with God. We went to the hospital, and they sent him to the ICU, where he stayed for the next month and a half.

I didn't have anyone to stay home with my babies this time. Y'all best believe I was calling that nursing station three times a day checking on Jr. because I didn't trust anyone to give me a true update on him. This was very hard on me. I remember going to visit and seeing death on him. I ran to a prayer partner's house and told her what I saw. She prayed with me, and God started speaking through her. He said I was His Angel; God kept saying this over and over. She said, "I don't know what that means, but He kept saying it." After we finished praying, I returned to the hospital, where no one was there except Dad White. He let me spend some time with Jr. by myself. Then the Lord took me to His word that said, "I choose to perform miracles, but because of the lack of FAITH, I can't." I cried, and I cried, but I still believed. God had shown me that his family didn't have TRUE FAITH. See, TRUE FAITH has NO PLAN B. The only plan that can work is plan A, *period.*

Jr. started having complications; his heart was weakening, he had become septic, and he was so full of fluid that it was coming out of his pores all over his body. But despite what it LOOKED like, my godmother taught us that as long as blood is running warm in our veins, anything is possible. I had made up my mind that I didn't care if Jr. was laying there like a dried-up prune; God could still heal him. By this time, I was staying with him, and his family members had to rotate because I couldn't be there day and night. It started getting hard on me, but I still trusted God, went to church, and worshiped Him like never before.

One mid-day, I went to check on Jr. to ensure he was only getting dialysis every other day (not back to back like they almost did one day). When I went up to the hospital, I saw that they had him on dialysis and shouldn't have because he had just had it a day before. Well, of course, I went *off*. The nurses just looked at me. Then the doctor and this one family member asked me to come into another room.

This family member then told me, "The FAMILY and I have decided not to resuscitate Jr. We think it's time to let him go." I must have looked at this person and said, "What GOD do you serve, and who are we to take his life? I'm not signing NOTHING! If God wants to take him, He doesn't need our help." As we went back and forth, I got called to his room. I was told that he was fading away. Now I'm looking at them because I see them put stuff in his IV to help him pass. I ran, jumped behind his bed, and laid my forehead on his forehead. I kept saying, *"I still believe. Don't give up, honey, don't give up; there is still hope."* I saw him crying. The tears were rolling down his face as he was fading away from us. I kept telling him, "Fight, baby, fight..." then, I saw him take his last breath.

They *killed* him!!! They pulled the plug on him behind my back. They told me to sign some papers right after he passed away so I couldn't come back and sue the hospital. *Is that even legal?* I was under duress; I was numb. Like, Jr. had just died, plus I was dealing with all the trauma from before and after our marriage. This was *a lot*. After Jr. passed, his family wanted to plan the funeral. I hardly had any say in it; my girls and I were hurting really bad. At this point, I didn't even know how to feel. So much had been said and done to me, but I still loved and trusted God like never before.

We didn't have an open casket, but we did have a nice service. Y'all ready for this? *Nawww, yall not ready...his family* and I were at the funeral home getting the cost of the casket, when they asked me about a life insurance policy. I didn't know whether my policy would be enough. We had gotten life insurance to help his brother with his new business venture six months before his death. I didn't know anything about the policy or how it worked. So, his brother told the other family members how much the policy was and had the guy that did our policy look into whether they would pay it out. In the meantime, Dad White says they would cover the burial. His wife said to me, "You can just pay us back." Dad says, "No, you don't," and she said, "Yes. Pay us back when you get the money."

Can y'all believe this? Like, she had a policy on him too. SMH. So, we paid, picked out the casket and decided on all that came with the package. That is the only part I played in the service—except, I asked if the worship group at our church would sing 'Gloried' (that was Jr. and I's favorite song). That song was so anointed. It's amazing how no one from his family came and checked on us to see if we were okay. However, the assistant pastor and a few church members checked on us regularly.

We finally had the service on Nov 22nd, 2008. He died on November 17th, 2008. We had a really nice service for him.

Bishop Holcomb (rest his soul—I just loved him), got up there and started talking and validating me as Jr.'s wife. Then (y'all ready for this?) he kept saying that I was *Jr.'s Angel.* He started talking about how good of a wife and mother I was. He said so many great things about me; it just brought me to tears. I was so numb from all I had been through; I had numb emotions. It was hard for me to even cry. My girls were hurt as well. Then I was mad at God: He gave me a son with no father after talking to him about not wanting to care for another child by myself. Now don't get it twisted; that lil boy is my everything. He kept me going.

About a week or so later, I remember sitting in our living room, and I felt Jr.'s presence. He was angry—like furious. I told him, "Don't be mad at me. I didn't pull the plug on you. Go to this particular family member. I fought to keep you alive." Now you would think that things were over??? NOOO, they weren't.

After I had gotten the money from the policy, my bishop at the time got really involved. He told me that it was not a lot of money and that I had to watch how I spent it. In the meantime, the Holy Spirit told me, "Do not tithe your money to the church." I was like, *huh*?? He said, "Yes. Don't tithe your money to the church." They were in debt. Now you would think that God would want me to help them out. He said, "No," a few times because God knows I would have tithed and given an offering. He had told me something about what was happening behind closed doors: money was being mismanaged. The bishop tried to take me to his bank so that I would give to the church. However, God showed me the agenda behind him taking me to the church's bank; so, I didn't.

Let me tell you, when I didn't tithe to them, I started getting a different kind of treatment. I had tithed to those who needed help. One person had a hole in the floor of their house, so I gave them money for repairs. I also helped a couple get a car. I just started helping people in need. I paid cash for a house for my children and me and remodeled it. Jr. had paid off my car before he passed, so I didn't have a car payment. His car payment was written off because of the way he had gotten his loan. We weren't married long enough for me to inherit his debt.

I just *lived a little*. I was ready to get back into the swing of things at church because I was still involved. I was a licensed minister that was ready to serve again. Every time I asked to come and volunteer at the church, the bishop's wife would tell me *no. I just needed to stay home.* I would tell her this was too much idle time and that I wanted to start serving again. I used to go to the church during the day to help with things when I wasn't working. This kept me out of trouble and prevented me from meeting the wrong people since I was still hurting. I had been so faithful, not just in service but in tithe and offering as well. I remember we had a women's encounter, and I attended because I needed a release from everything I had gone through. Man, that encounter was powerful.

I remember Pastor Holy ministered to me and said, "I know you're not ready to hear this, but God has a husband for you. God showed me who this person was, and I asked God to allow us to talk; that He would create a situation that would put us in the same room." And God did just that. So, I asked this person if Pastor Holy came to them. This person said yes, she did. However, he had told her he couldn't do it. Then he told me that he didn't want a wife that was a minister; he wanted a wife that was a virgin who supported his ministry. I wasn't offended by it at all. I learned that God could have someone for you, but that person had a right to choose you or not since they have free will. So, we remained friends and never talked about it again.

After the encounter, I called the church again, asking to come down to help. I was told no again. This time I told her I had too much idle time and wanted to serve, so I didn't get caught up—I was too vulnerable. Pastor D told me no, I needed to stay home, grieve, and give myself time. Guess what happened?? I met someone who was a firefighter. We got along great. Then we started dating. He filled a void that I was trying to fill by serving, and because I was told no, I couldn't come serve, I met this young man.

At this point, I was still attending church and serving God with my entire heart wanting more of Him. So, another woman's encounter came up. I volunteered to be a small group leader. The bishop's wife called me and said, "I see that you signed up to be a small group leader; but, you're in a relationship, and we take encounters seriously." Now mind you, the person who was over-officiating the encounters was one of the ministers who spoke during an encounter. Her boyfriend was living with her and *everyone* knew this. So I told her, "I guess your sin is overlooked if your gift is needed???" She didn't have anything to say about that. From that point, I started seeing the church differently: the issue was I didn't pay my tithes to them. They were upset about it.

One day, I went to a service. I was about to put money in the basket when the Holy Spirit said, "Do not give." I was like, "*What*??? Don't give…up???" He said no to me as loud as day. I was like, *why would the Holy Spirit tell me not to give?* Then God told me to remove myself from the ministry. I was like, *huh*??? My girls started asking questions. They were mad at God, saying, "After you've been so faithful to a church, why would God allow any of these things to happen to you?" I tried to explain, but it was hard at the time. So, I ended up leaving the church. At this time, I didn't know that the assistant pastor was stepping down. We didn't talk like that.

Y'all ready for this? Now there was a rumor that my assistant pastor and I were seeing each other!? *What in the Sam Hill*? Like, are you serious right now? We had the purest pastor and lay member relationship. He was the ONLY one that was there for me and really prayed for me while going through the process with Jr. We talked all the time. He kept me sane.

That's not all. The rumor was that he and I embezzled money from the church. I was like, *what???* Jr. and I had life insurance policies; that's how I received the money I had. This devastated me even more. I was a FAITHFUL tither and gave more than I had in offering for the seven years I was there. It was like one hit after another. I was like, "God forget this mess. See, I'd rather go to the streets and minister because if it's a dog, it's going to bark, and if it's a cat, it'll say meaoowoooo." In rage and with tears running down my face, I told God to strip me of EVERY OUNCE of religion. I didn't care who prophesied what about me and who said what I was going to be. "I want to know YOU GOD, for MYSELF! Show me who I am in You. *You* show *me.* You reveal what I'm supposed to be," I said to Him. I was so hurt.

I remember it like it was yesterday: it was late at night. I know it was Saturday because the next day was Sunday. God told me to wake up and turn on the Potter's House which usually started at 9 am on Sundays. I was like, "Bishop doesn't come on until eleven in the morning," and then turned over to continue sleeping. God said, "I said *get up,* and turn on the Potter's House *right now.* He has a word for you." I was still upset and really didn't want to watch any church things. So, lo and behold, I logged on just as the bishop was saying, "If you logged on today, I don't just have a *word*—I have a *Word* from the Lord." I was like, *wow, okay God.*

I watched the service. I don't remember the title, but the Holy Spirit hit me; a whale cry came to let me know it was God.

The bishop talked to someone in their bed, and they received the Holy Spirit. I just really broke after that. Once service was over, God took me to a Scripture I'll never forget: Jeremiah 3:15, "And I will give you pastors according to my own heart, and they shall feed you with knowledge and understanding." This is when my healing began, and a new journey started…

CONCLUSION

God Didn't Hurt You

A lot of the people I spoke of in this book were those who I expected to love me because they were my mother, father, or sibling. Others I expected to exemplify love because they professed their love for God or were a messenger or a leader sent by God. Like most of you, I stopped trusting human leadership because of everything I had encountered. After my spiritual mother passed away, I sought a leader to develop what I felt God was calling me to do.

Back then, being pretty didn't make it any better for me. I was taught to always speak to the woman of God and go to her for anything I needed, including prayer. No matter how much I applied this teaching, wives became intimidated by me. I was like, "Lord, I don't even see what they see." As a matter of fact, for a long time, I always thought I was ugly. The more I tried to make it right, the worse it became so much that I started to feel like an outcast.

My desire for someone to teach me how to become what God had called me to do became a tormenting fight. Then after being hurt by that which I desired so much (spiritual mother/

father), I didn't realize I wanted what I had in Madea: to be understood, loved unconditionally, and corrected with love. The desire was so strong that it turned into wanting to be validated by man, more than God, because I wanted to do God's will right. I was looking for God to validate me through a man/human being, but didn't have any idea what that looked like. God showed me the leaders' sins and had me pray and cover them no matter what I saw. If I noticed a weakness, I would pray for it not to be revealed because I was taught that you should pray for your leader and whatever you see in them or anyone else; pray that if it is in you, then God should deliver you too.

I realized that I had a false expectation because they were imperfect people that had experienced trauma and were trying to figure things out on their own—imperfect vessels of God that were human. God allowed things to happen to qualify me for the call of God that is in my life. He had to teach me the DO's and the DON'Ts on how not to treat His people once He placed me in the position He had called me to. What does that look like? I still have no idea; I'm just taking notes. LOL!

One day, I got mad at God and said, "You know they are accusing me falsely. What they're saying about me is not my spirit nor a true word they are speaking. You call these your men and women of God? Why aren't You revealing the truth?" I'll never forget what He said as I mentioned in a previous chapter. I heard His voice as clear as someone standing next to me. He said, "SO YOU WILL KNOW HOW NOT TO TREAT MY

PEOPLE." Then I started realizing that He was teaching me how to be HIS leader; reflecting His ways through the things He allowed me to suffer and see. He taught me what true prophecy was, and what discernment was that people referred to as prophecy. Those that were speaking from a place of discernment could only see the residue on one's life. The one speaking from the mouth of God prophesied based on one's heart posture (God showed them the HEART).

When God started teaching me these things, I realized He didn't hurt me; he was just developing my leadership skills, birthing a pastor's heart, and teaching me to love unconditionally. He was teaching me relationship vs. religion-ship (I made this word up). It wasn't religion He was teaching me or you. He taught and is teaching me not to have a Pharisee spirit (research what a pharisee spirit is), just like He has been developing you all this time.

As you can see, God didn't do any of these things to you. If He allowed it, know that He thought so highly of you that He knew you would get through it, and become His great servant one day. The enemy would love for you to have a false perception and make you question that which you believe. Don't believe in religion; believe in Jesus. Believe in God, who is the Author and Finisher of your faith; your Redeemer, your will in the middle of the will, your bright and morning star, your mind regulator, your Prince of Peace, your Elohim (YOUR GOD). He loves you; He'll cleanse you. He'll wash you white as snow. You could have been dead right now. It was God that kept you. It was God that told death to behave. It was God who made you different from your whole family so you could break the curse that's been there for years. Don't let the devil steal your faith.

I know you can't see it right now, but He loves you. He loves you so much that you can talk to him high, drunk, or laying in the bed with someone else's spouse. You could have murdered someone; you might be a witch or a warlock. God loves you too. The devil will have you saying, "I don't believe in religion." Yet, he will have you worshiping crystals, sage, and card readers telling you you need to be washed. Indirectly, he'll make a covenant for you to be free but instead, your family will be bound by the devil.

You may be the one that became a card reader because the church failed to teach you about your gifts and what TRUE spirituality is (not this false spirituality that is borderline witchcraft). God is the only God that has supernatural powers. The evil spirits of this world attempt to emulate it by using the gift that GOD gave you for evil. Satan can make you do this through unforgiveness, bitterness, envy, strife, through your bloodline, or the lack of knowledge.

God protected my mind when the spirit of suicide was talking louder than my voice. So much that I was in my bed lying down in a fetus position calling on Jesus because the voice was getting louder and louder. My son came into my room on a Wednesday night and said, "Mom, let's go to church; you need to go worship." I got up, put on a hat, and pleaded the blood of Jesus over my mind all the way there. I called a pastor

I knew, crying, asking him to please pray for me. The voice of suicide was louder than my voice. As I hung up, the voice got faint and eventually went away as I worshiped every day at home.

God is a keeper. He said he would be our strength in the midst of our weakness. It's what He has consistently done for me and for you! :) God loves you and wants you to come to Him today. You don't have to tell anyone. This is between you and God. He will give you a way out of witchcraft; He will deliver you out of the mafia. I don't know who this is for, but God said He's going to let you out of jail, give you a chance to serve Him for real, and make you wealthy. If you don't, you will die by the same hands you sinned with.

For every fallen leader that may read this book, God is calling you back to your rightful position. He doesn't care what you have done, and who doesn't think you are qualified. God says, "Come now, for I, thy God, will wash you. Come to Me as you are. You don't need a building; you NEED Me. For I AM THE CHURCH, and I, thy GOD, live in your HEART. There will be no inkling of sin on you or in you. Tell Me yes now, and watch Me move on you like I once used to when you spent time with Me. I will show you the way and the path. Cleanse yourself from all unrighteousness, for now is the hour for Me to vindicate you. For your suffering was not in vain. I know why you did what you did and I AM thy God who forgiveth thee. I am reconciling My children back to Me."

Right now, I want you to meditate and think about all you have been through from a different perspective (with tears running down your face). I know it hurts. I used to cry, and cry, and cry so much I had tear stains on my face. However, I never turned my heart away from God. Take this time to pray and let God have His way with you right now. If you are coming to Christ for the first time, just say, "Lord, I believe in my heart and confess with my mouth that I receive Jesus Christ as my personal Lord and Savior." Let the Lord know you can't do this on your own. Tell Him you would like to have an encounter with Him to assure you that He is real so no one could ever tell you He isn't. Ask for a supernatural encounter with Him and His angels.

If you need protection, read Psalms 91, and you'll believe God will protect you. If you are being falsely accused, pray Psalms 35. If you want to be a woman of God, read and add your name to Psalms 31. If you want to be a man of God, insert your name into Ephesians 5. Then for everyone, read Isaiah 55.

Know that God loves you, looks beyond your faults and sees your needs. He's just waiting on you to open your heart and let Him in. *God Didn't Hurt You*—man's imperfect and dysfunctional ways did. For God is a God of hope and reconciliation. Let Him reconcile you back to Him today. Let the Lord into your heart. Jeremiah 29:11-13 says, "For I know the plans I have for you," declares the LORD, "plans to prosper you and not to harm you, plans to give you hope and a future. Then you will call on me and come and pray to me, and I will listen to you. You will seek me and find me when you seek me with all your heart."

For God so loved the world that He gave His ONLY begotten son, that whoever believes in him shall not perish but have everlasting life (John 3:16). This is how much God loves you and me.

The Cry Of The Soul

Hello.

Can anyone see what's going on inside?

I hope someone will take my hand and
help me stand while I struggle with the old man.

A wave of water blew out my fire,
but my spirit man still desired to go on.

But, the storm seemed so long, and I became
weak and lost myself.

Watch out! A snake bit me and grabbed a hold,
but God was still in control.

The bride is waiting for the groom,
hoping I'll someday leave this gloom.

That's when the spirit rekindles the fire,
and encourages the bride to inspire others
to hold on; to not give up.

God is like Folgers: He will send someone to
fill your cup.

He will let you know you're not alone;
you can overcome it as a sign that God saw
your crying soul.

TIA

ACKNOWLEDGMENT

First, I want to give honor to God, who has graced me to do what I never thought I could do. I'm so humbled and would do anything He asked me to do through His strength. The saying I have adopted is, *"If God isn't going to be there, I don't want it."*

I thank God for the relationship I have with my mother and father. You are amazing, supportive, and encouraging. Life challenges tried to divide us, but God's strength has given me the ability to forgive and understand you instead of condemning you. He has allowed me to see the amazing Parents and friends you are today. I love you oooh so dearly!! I'm honored to be your daughter.

I want to thank Hydeia for believing in me. Thank you for taking an entire day to sit and listen to my story, and helping me with the titles and outlines of my book. It's because of God's gifts in you that have allowed me to not only start but finish my book. I have never been a writer, however, I have done my best to obey God's voice when he tells me to do something. So, thank you for helping me to obey the voice of God and challenging my fears until my book was completed.

www.ingramcontent.com/pod-product-compliance
Lightning Source LLC
Chambersburg PA
CBHW050516160726
48003CB00001B/329